# Albany History Reader

## Volume One

### Don Rittner

Dedicated to
Kevin J. Rittner

ISBN: 978-0-03-766669-2

©2022 Don Rittner
All Rights Reserved

No part of this publication may be reproduced, stored in a retrieval system, or transmitted in any form or by any means, electronic, mechanical, photocopying, recording, or otherwise without prior permission.

Published by
New Netherland Press
Schenectady NY

# Table of Contents

Introduction, 1

The Albany Plan Of Preservation, 3

Albany's History Of Destroying Its History, 25

Don't Judge A Book By Its Cover (Or A Building By Its Facade), 35

What Do You Do When You Find The Roots Of Your Historic City, 59

Such Promise But No Vision, 63

Another Removal of Albany History Hits The Road, 69

Welcome to the Albany Historium, 77

Boiling Plant threatens The Most important Archaeological Site in the Northeast United States, 91

The Albany Greenbelt Revisited, 95

North Dakota's Crude Trick On Albany, 103

Boiling Plant Should Be Designed For Any Possibility, 107

Preserve Fort Nassau, and Fort Nassau 2, and Fort Nassau 3, and…, 113

Will the Real Fort Nassau Please Stand Up!, 119

We Need A 2020 "New Deal" Public Works Program, 131

Welcome to Albany's Renaissance Hotel, 157

New Renaissance Hotel Honors The History of the Old DeWitt Clinton, 181

A Landslide Of Uncommon Sense, 189

Honey, I Have A Sinking Feeling About This, 192

Dear Albany, Why?, 198

Top. Albany looking west on June 12, 1951. Bottom. Albany looking east on June 2, 1948. New York State Archives.

# Introduction

For twenty years (1999 to 2007 - 2009 to 2021), I wrote a local history-centered column that appeared in the Troy Record and the Albany Times Union newspapers in the Capital District region of New York State. During these two decades, I tried to educate the public on the unique history that makes up the region since it was here that American history began when the Dutch built a small fur trading fort on an island in 1614, now part of the City of Albany, the present Capital of the State.

In these two decades, local politics has allowed the continual destruction of much of our valuable archaeological, historic, and ecological sites. While I wish I could say it is uncommon, as you will see from reading these articles, it has been the standard operating procedure for the oldest continually European-settled area in the United States. Native Americans called it home for thousands of years until displaced by events of the 18th century. They lived in harmony with the environment. Not so with the later European mentality that proclaims the Earth and its resources are for the taking, no matter the cost.

Many articles feature ideas that could have increased tourism and tax base if followed. However, politics in the Capital District is four centuries old and harbors a collected disdain for its history. It seems to be prevalent in the minds of those who get elected. Frustrating, to say the least.

In this ancient area, you should expect to find a great deal of history to uncover and write about. Many writers before me have done so and many will in the future. Why is history important? Knowing it can save one from making the same mistakes. It only takes burning your hand on the stove one time to realize that it is precious information and will make you think twice about doing it again. Knowing history allows you to understand your place in the evolution of humanity. It is inescapable. Every human creates their individual history and collectively provides information that can help move us forward. Knowing the history, especially your local history, provides a sense of place, a familiarity, or security of mind, when you go about your daily life. The more I learn about my neighborhood more secure I feel living in it.

So here I am republishing a selection of my stories that I feel are useful or interesting during a time of uncertainty. Volume One contains articles that deal with the early history of Albany and some ideas on how to capitalize on this history to increase heritage tourism and showcase the contributions Albany has made to American history in the last four centuries.

Albany, at one time called the "City on the Pine Plains," is surrounded by nature. I can think of no other 400-year-old American City that still has original wilderness surrounding it. You will learn about the Albany Greenbelt, an idea to incorporate this fact into a hiking and bike trail around the city. You will also find a story about digging up downtown and turning it into an archaeological park which would draw thousands of visitors to Albany. You will also learn about historic preservation efforts and successes like the restoration of the DeWitt Clinton Hotel and the battles to prevent the destruction of early archaeological sites, including Fort Nassau, the first European structure built in New York State. Volume Two of this "History Reader" series deals with 19th-century Albany. It includes articles about the controversy over the possible removal of a Revolutionary War Hero's statue, Albany's connection to the killing of Abraham Lincoln and Houdini, and the plan to create the first underwater tunnel connecting Albany to the city of Rensselaer.

History changes by the day. One can only hope that what you do today will be looked back on as a contribution to the progress of human society so that its eventual final chapter can be one that made it worth its existence. Illustrations are from my collection, public domain, or otherwise listed.

Don Rittner
July 2022

Albany Seal

# The Albany Plan (of Preservation)
First published on July 16, 2012 12:36 pm

*"Albany, city of my birth! Ancient, yet new! Replete with interesting associations of the past, connected by so many links with the present, and promising to posterity a glorious future. They antique dwellings have been leveled, not so much by the hand of Time, as the merciless spirit of improvement.*

*Goths and Vandals! Ye were the sweet dispensers of the charities of life, compared to the demon who now stalks abroad under that abused name.*

*Where now are the palaces of the Knickerbockers and the Van Winkles? Gone! Leveled with the dust, or oh! Worse, far worse, modernized!*

*Why the very Holland bricks — if they could speak, would cry shame! And the substantial beams fall down and crush the walls in their deep despair, when they are subjected to the degrading process of modernizing!*

*Shades of our fathers! Why is it permitted? To renovate, to preserve those remnants of the past, should be our pious aim, not with profane hands to cut, hew down, and alter the roof trees which have sheltered generation after generation."*

-------**The Monthly Rose, Albany Female Academy, 1845**

**Preserving Albany's Undiscovered City**

More than ten years ago, Albany historian John Wolcott and myself, along with input from Steve Comer, then representing the Stockbridge-Munsee Band of Mohicans, prepared an extensive report called **The Albany Plan of Preservation** in an effort to call attention to the rich buried archeological resources of Albany. We were hoping we could interest the elected officials of the city to see the importance of preserving this unique prehistory and European history that was buried beneath the streets. Obviously it fell on deaf ears but considering there is a proposal to build a civic center in downtown I thought this would be as good a time as ever to polish off the report and update and present it here for everyone to read.

More than 200 years ago, at the urging of the Iroquois Nation, representatives from the original colonies met in Albany to create a **Plan of Union** (1754). It is now time once more to meet in Albany, at the urging of interested citizens, to create a new plan -- the **Albany Plan of Preservation**.

Beneath the paved streets and footprints of hundreds of buildings in downtown Albany lies an ancient city and its inhabitants eager to tell a story.

For more than 350 years, early settlers from a variety of countries eked out a life in the Albany area. For thousands of years before them, Mohican Indians and their ancestors lived in harmony with Albany's environment. Both have left evidence of their lives and times eager to reveal their story about Albany as they knew it.

However, as we uncover these bits of insight into our past, developers and politicians quickly rebury them, almost embarrassed at the discovery of such important finds. They allow archaeologists a few moments of time to sift through the rubble trying to patch together enough of the story — but are always one step ahead of waiting bulldozers ready to sweep the story back into the depths in which they were found. It seems there never is enough time for our history — an odd paradox.

In the last few years, sections of Albany's protective stockade have been uncovered. Skeletons of former inhabitants have been awakened from their peace. Foundations of early homes and businesses have been mapped and trinkets and treasures owned by Native and European alike recorded and cataloged. Launching points for sloops seeking out the unknown chartered waters of the world have been photographed. Most of these are "accidental" or incidental discoveries as a result of activities in the name of 'progress.' But where are these treasures now? Reburied with parking garages and commercial office towers sitting on top of them. This is progress? No, this is regress! These are actions that are economic suicide.

**Creating the Beverwyck Archeological Park**

Albany has an opportunity to develop itself into a successful and profitable heritage destination center for the 21st century, or it can continue to bow to the needs of a few myopic profit driven business ventures and fade into a third class 'citycenship.' There needs to be a coordinated and detailed excavation, preservation, and promotion of Albany's underground resources. Standing historic structures should not be ignored either and should become part of a redevelopment effort rather than torn down. There is a unique opportunity to create a downtown archaeological park unlike any in the United States, and perhaps the world.

Instead of the usual run of the mill exhibits behind glass cases, or bronze plagues marking where history formerly stood, Albany has a chance to design a unique below and above ground living museum where visitors can see and experience Albany's history in place.

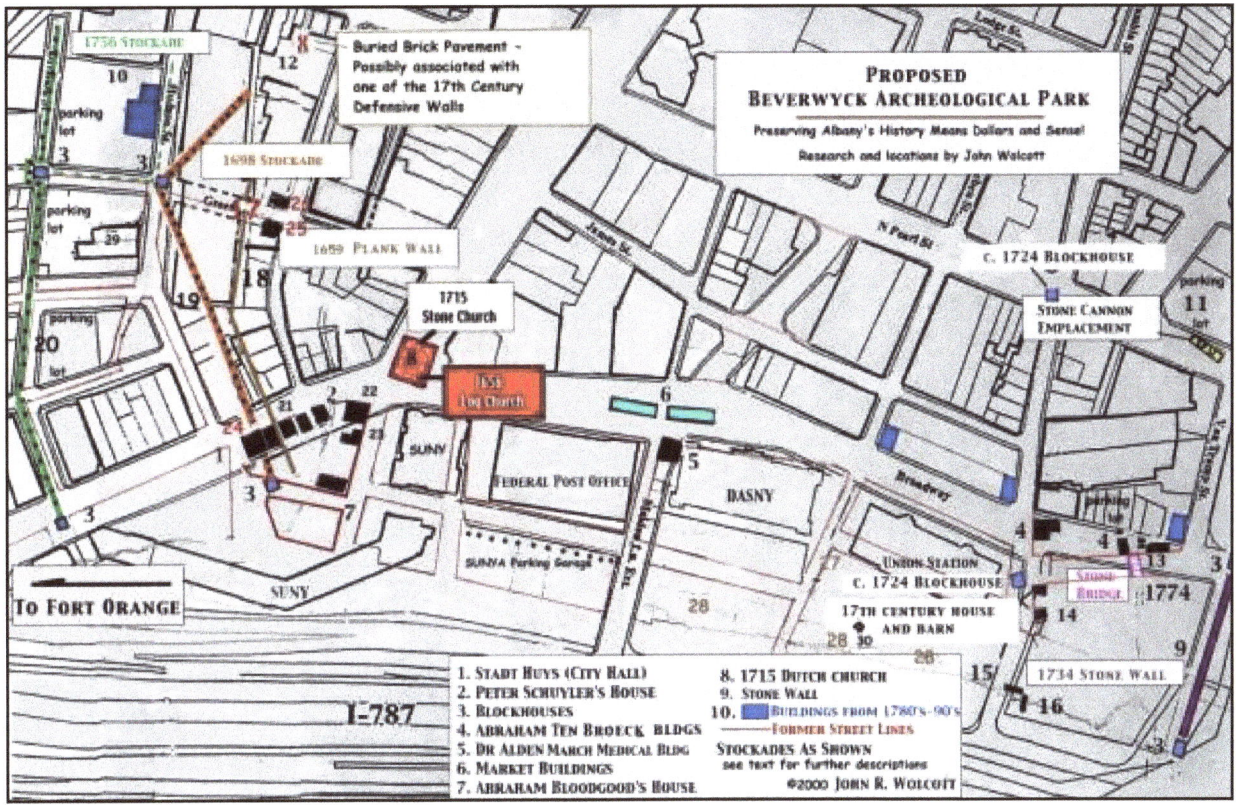

Underground Albany Map as prepared by Don Rittner and John Wolcott in 2000.

As luck or fate would have it, many of Albany's most important archeological treasures are presently located beneath streets, parks, or parking lots, NOT buildings, making their excavations possible.

We have pinpointed these awaiting discoveries.

Over a dozen sites are ready to be excavated and tied into a connected archaeological park which we call **Beverwyck Archeological Park** and which represent much of the earliest European and Native habitation of Albany.

The following sites are waiting to be rediscovered (See numbers on the map):

1. The Stadt Huys. This building was the center for Albany's regional government which included Albany, Schenectady, Niskayuna, Half Moon, Catskill, and Kinderhook and was created when the British administration took over the area in 1664. Also called the "Coenings Huys," or "King's House."
State House, City Hall.

The State House.

To the Mohawk, and likely the Mohicans, this place was very important because it was the locale for many of their conferences with colonial officials. The leader of the Maquaas (Mohawk) made a speech in this house in 1689 at the opening of the King Williams War, when the English were seeking their alliance against the French.

On the map you can see the part of the city hall which is north of the city wall. This was the first part built. It was appropriated for the use of the village government circa 1665. The second part of the building south of the wall is an addition and rebuilding in 1740.

2. Peter Schuyler's House. Schuyler bought the house in 1679 and was the first mayor of Albany under the charter of 1686. New York's Governors appointed the mayor of Albany for years. NY Indian Commissioner for several years.

3. Blockhouses. These were made with square timbers and had an overhanging second floor which had cannons and holes for muskets for defensive purposes and bunks for soldiers in them. There were located strategically around the stockades.

4. Abraham Ten Broeck's buildings. He was a representative on the NY Assembly in 1760 representing the Manor or Rensselaerwyck. He ran the Manor for Stephen Van Rensselaer III during his minor years beginning in 1769. In

Peter Schuyler. First mayor of Albany.

The Market buildings as painted by James Eights.

Albany in 1694 showing Dutch Church and buildings to the South (left). These are available for excavation.

1775, at the beginning of the Revolution, he was a solid Whig and served as the 3rd ward representative of the Albany Committee of Safety and was elected to the NY Provincial Congress. In 1776, he was elected President of the State Congress and was a delegate for the Continental Congress. He was also the president of the convention that framed the first NYS Constitution. Finally he served as a Brigadier General and played an important role at the Battle at Saratoga. He was Mayor of Albany twice. The building on the South side of the kill may be the wagon house and moved to his new mansion in 1798.

5. Dr. Alden March Medical Office. March sub-leased the building in 1832 from Dr. Thos. Hun, who was in Paris, but had agents running his affairs in Albany. Dr. March rented this 18th century house and altered it for medical practice with other doctors and to practice anatomy lessons there which led him to found the Albany Medical

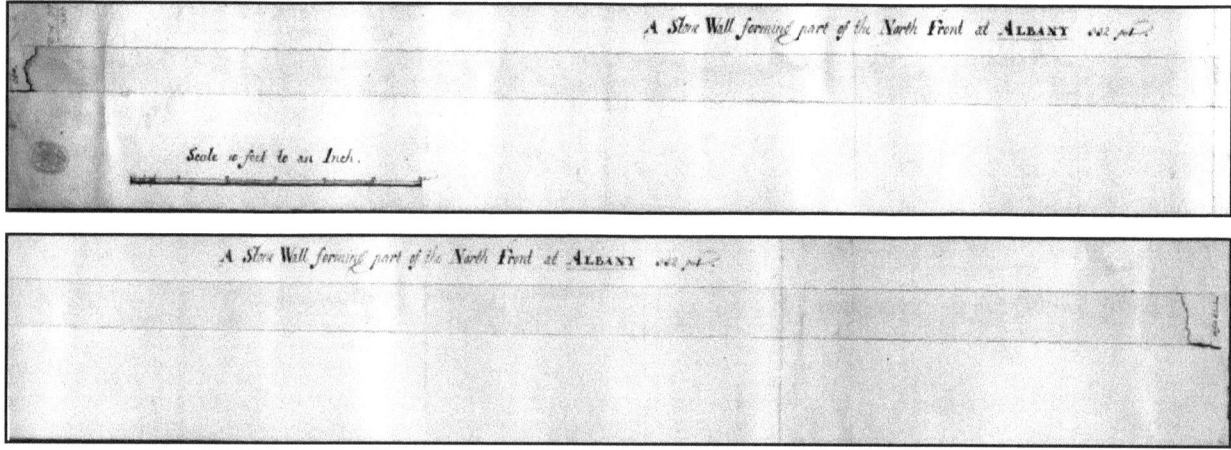

Albany Stone wall profile (top and bottom).

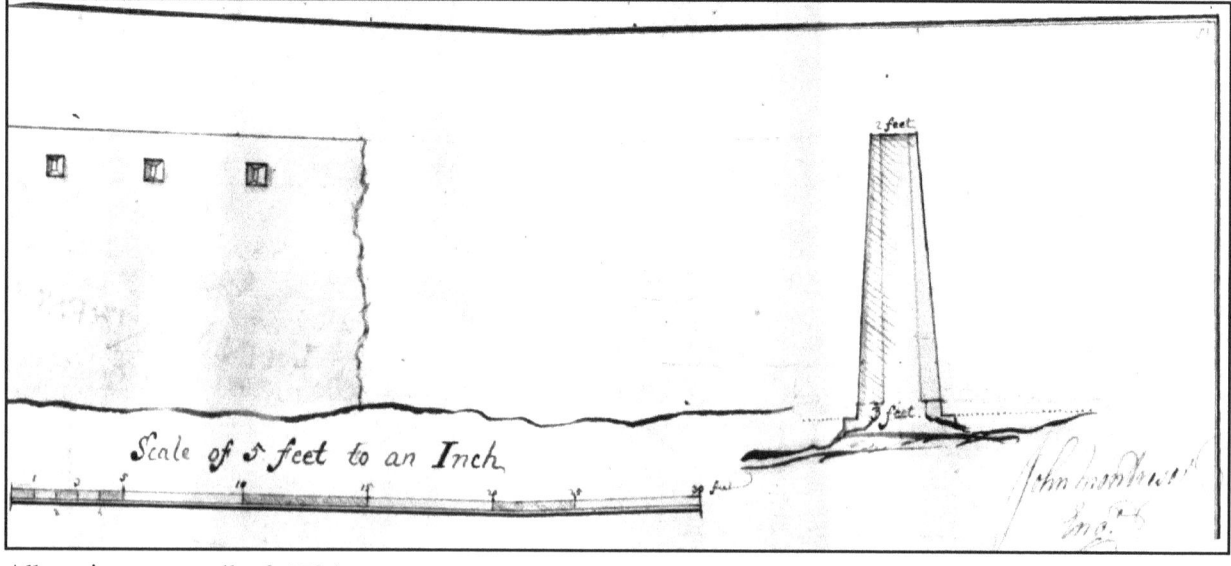

Albany's stone wall of 1734.

College. The building was razed when they widened this block of Maiden Lane by 33 feet on the north side in 1836.

6. Market buildings. These were pavilions for meat and produce vendors and maintained by the city for the public. This was known as the Third Ward Market House. While two locations are shown, it is the same building. The Simeon DeWitt manuscript map of 1790 shows it in the middle of market street just to the north side of Maiden Lane. The better known printed map of Simeon De Witt of 1794 shows the building of same dimensions just on the south side of Maiden Lane. It appears the same building was moved south for some reason. James Eights depicts it in one of his famous paintings of downtown.

7. Prominent merchant Abraham Bloodgood's late 18th century house.

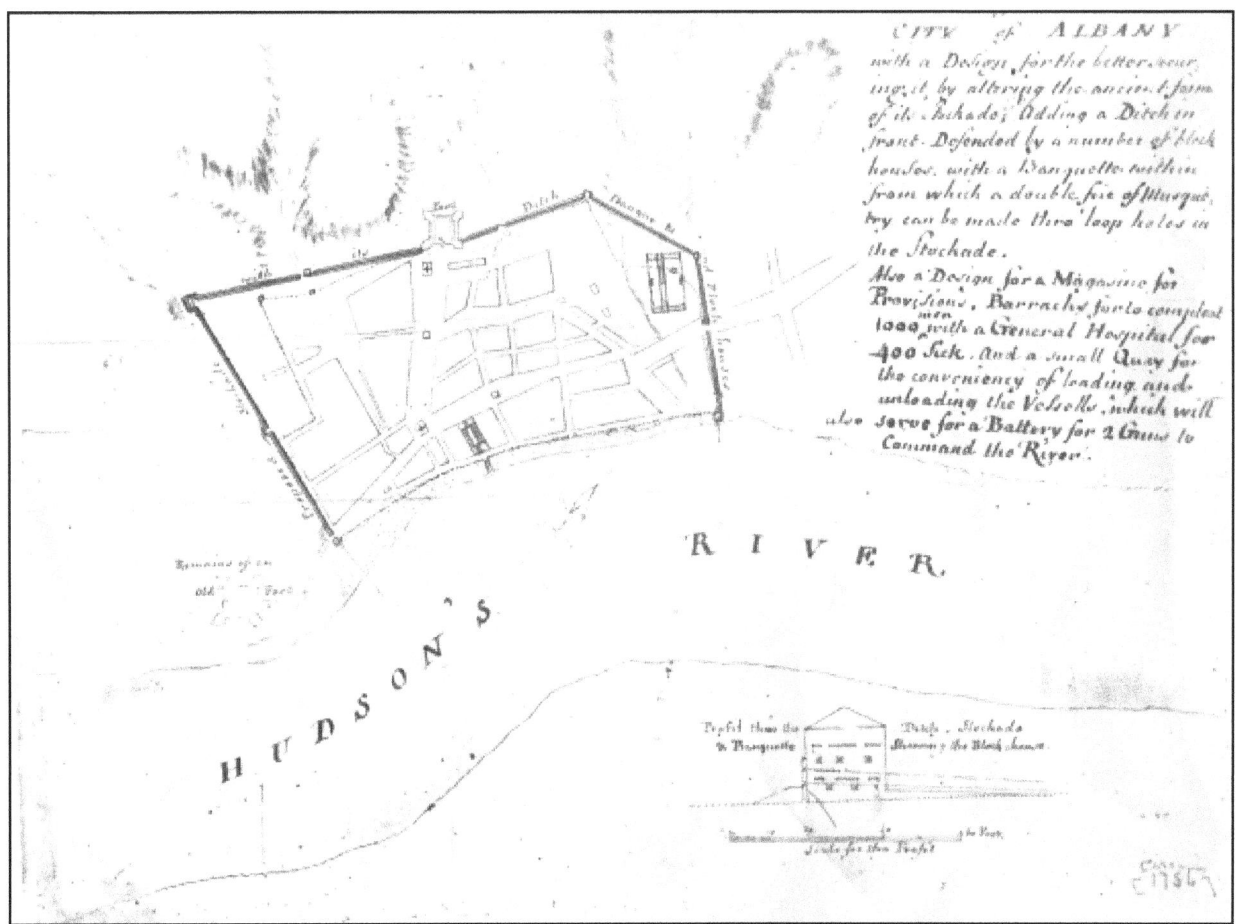

Albany in 1756 showing location of stockade, blockhouses, street plan and other structures.

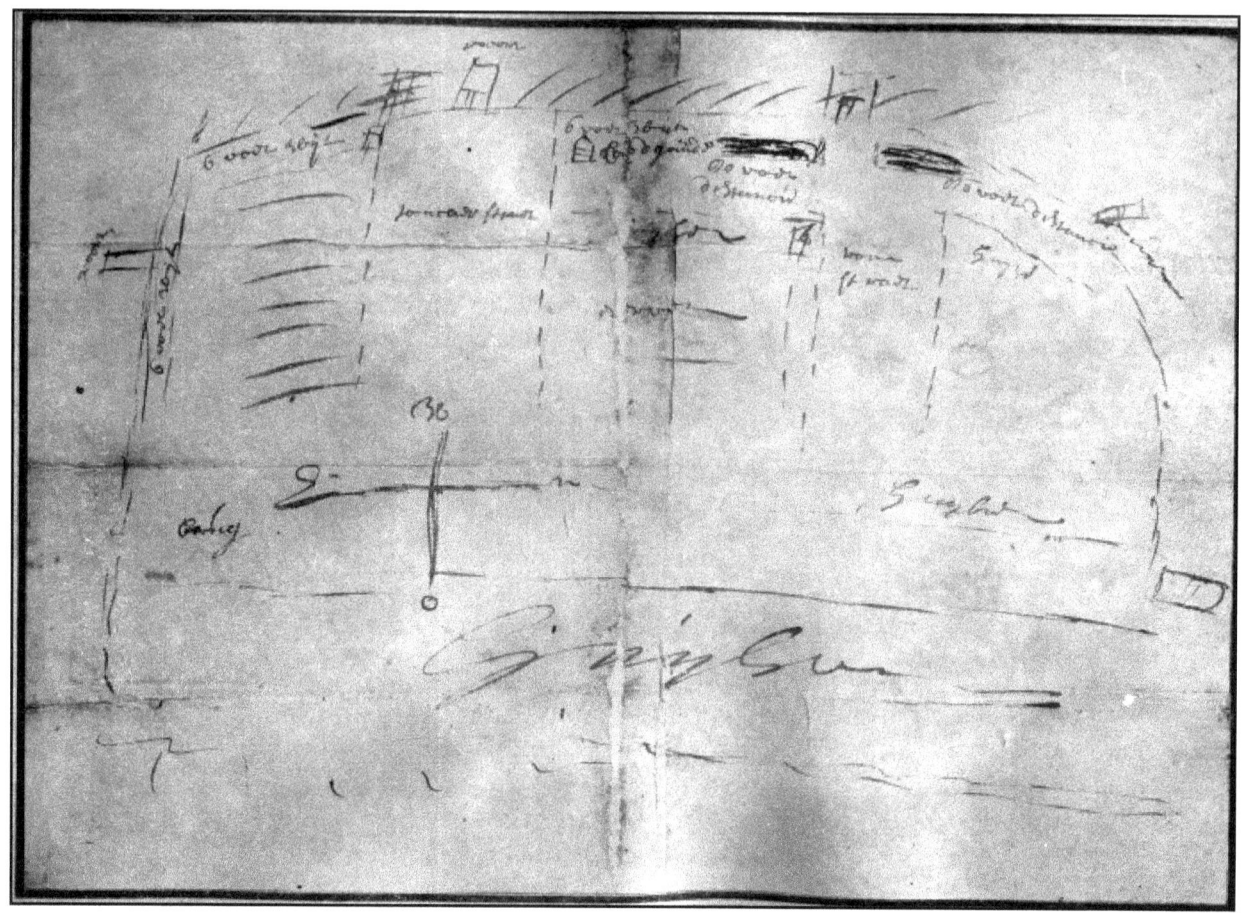

Number 18 on the map. 1659 Plank Wall. This is the first defensive wall built around Albany.

8. 1656 and 1715 Dutch Church (kerck). This was Albany's second church building (dash line) and was called blockhouse church. It had cannons in the tower. This was torn down and replaced with a larger stone church (solid line) in 1715.

9. City Wall (stone). Built in 1734 and originally projected to surround the entire city. Albany petitioned the NY Assembly to finance it on the premise that Albany was very important in the defense of the entire province. Only this portion from the river to the road to Watervliet (Broadway) was built. The area behind the wall became a street called Wall Street, now present day Orange Street. The NY legislature was too cheap to raise any more money to finish the wall. Final northern position of the city defenses.

10. Various buildings from 1780's-90's (Federal). Now demolished, but observed in the 1960s and 70's.

Part of the Albany Stockade uncovered off Broadway by archaeologists.

11. 1756 Stone Cannon Emplacement. Cannons were placed at the edge of ravines for defensive purposes.

12. Beaver Street site. Brick paving in 1999 on Omni development office building site. May be associated with the earliest Beverwyck defensive Wall. This feature is said to extend westerly under an adjoining small parking lot.

13. 1774 Stone Bridge. Crossed Vossen Kill. Timber bridge before.

14. 17th Century House and barn of Mees Hogeboom.

15. Fire Pit with mixed mid-17th century items of European and Indian trade items and artifacts.

16. Remains of a dock which locates the shoreline of the original Hudson River.

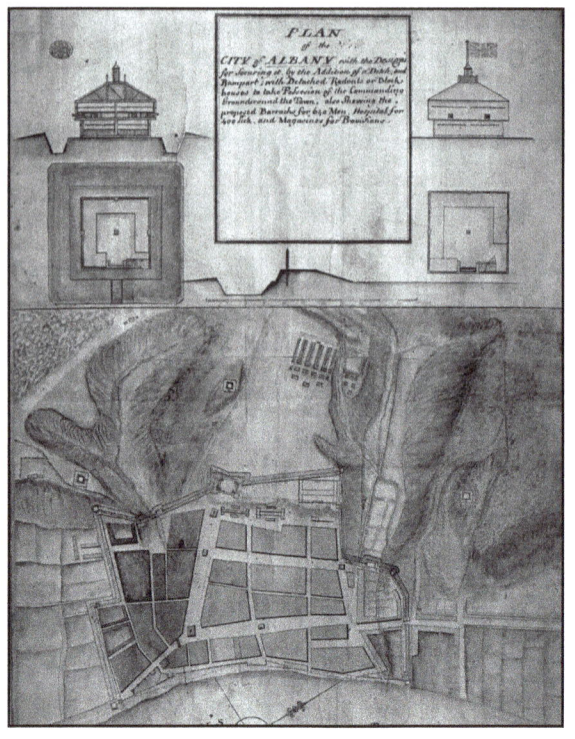

Blockhouses surrounded Albany and served as protection during conflict.

17. Slichtenhorst Gate. This was the only gate on the South side of original defensive wall of planks that was built in 1659. The North side of the passage of the current garage is in the same location.

18. 1659 Plank Wall. This is the first defensive wall built around Albany.

19. 1698 Stockade. This defensive stockade was up by 1698 (Romer Map, but probably built in 1671).

20. 1756 Stockade. This defensive stockade was up by 1756. Final southern position of city defenses.

The Dutch Church in the middle of State and Broadway. Painting by James Eights.

Albany stockade posts found by John Wolcott in downtown Albany.

Part of the Albany Stockade uncovered off Broadway by archeologists.

21. Two 17th century houses of William Loveridge, Master Hatter. The northern one was converted to, or replaced by a brew house by the end of the century.

22. Jochim Wessels, the Baker. 17th century.

23. Jurriaem Teunisse, the Glassmaker. 17th Century.

24. The South Gate of the Stockade probably 1671.

25. Hendrick van Dyck house - Albany Physician.

26. Lambert van Valkenburgh house.

27. A block of 17th and 18th century buildings. Foundations probably have survived under the garage floor. Early foundations of this block are also very likely to be found under the Northeast corner of Kiernan Way and between the city garage and Union Station.

28. Tackels Strant ("Strand" or "Beach").

29. Opportunity for above

Excavations of Fort Orange took place in 1970 but then covered up for the offramp of I-787.

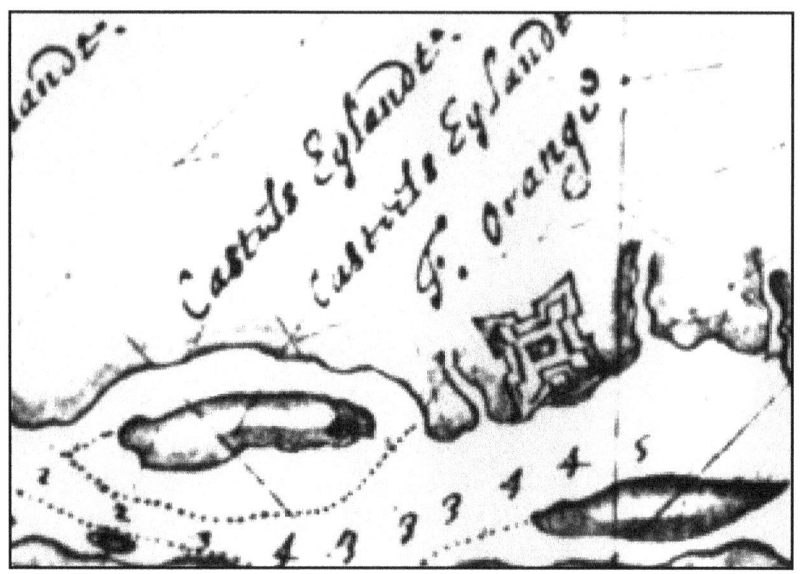

17th-century map showing the location of Fort Orange.

ground archeology - 48 Hudson, portion, ca. 1728; 50 Hudson, Federal Style, ca. 1808.

30. Roseboom's "Buyl Huys" (Bolting house) at Tackels Strant.

This is just a sample of sites that await rediscovery and preservation.

## Bringing Back Fort Orange

NOT ON THE MAP, but just east of and across from the current Holiday Inn Express lies the remains of Fort Orange, the original Albany. Buried under the North and south bound lanes and off ramp of Interstate 787 in 1968, this is one of the most important archeological sites in the United States.

It should become a priority to dismantle this road complex and re-excavate Fort Orange and make it the center of Albany's preservation efforts and the starting point for the Beverwyck Archeological Park. To have this most important piece of history covered by a mere and insignificant relict of the car culture is nothing less than a crime.

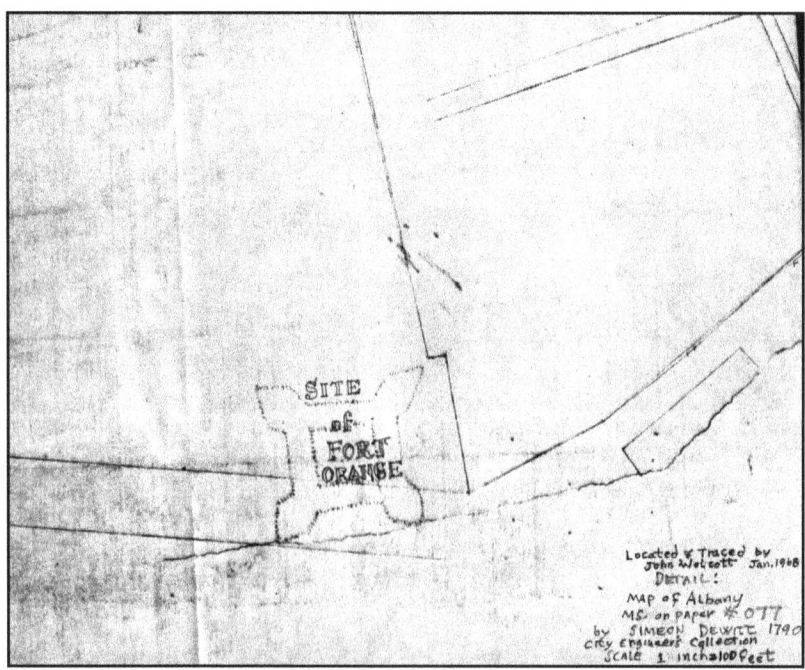

Local historian John Wolcott discovered the location of Fort Orange which later state archaeologists excavated.

## Create a Living Mohican Village

The land upon which Albany currently sits was

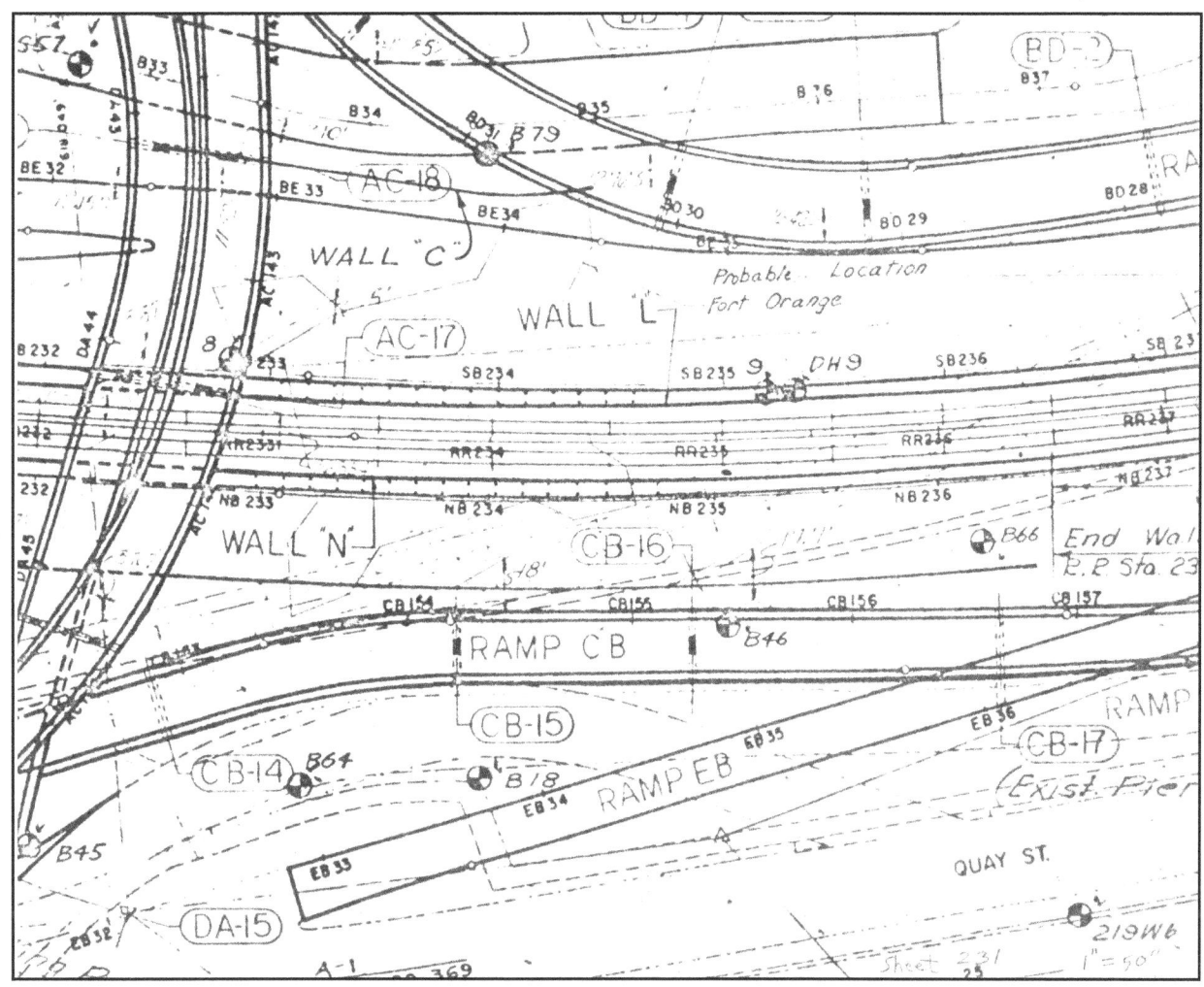
Fort Orange is buried under I-787 but a bastion is still available for excavation.

the ancestral home to the Algonquian speaking 'Muh-he ka-ne-ok' or Mahicans, today called the Mohicans, who were forced out the region in the early 1630s. These people were described as a "free, rich and well known nation," in 1634 when they were dealing with the Dutch here at 'Gastanek' (Albany).

The Mohicans, now called the Stockbridge-Munsee Band of Mohican Indians currently reside on a reservation in Wisconsin.

No one knows for sure when the Mohicans came into the region, but there is evidence that early man was in the Hudson Valley as early as 12,500 BC, hunting herds of caribou, with stone tipped spears, as they migrated up the Hudson Valley. Today, we know the Mohican people inhabited the Hudson River Valley from the Catskill Mountains north to the southern end of Lake Champlain, west to the Schoharie River region extending east to the Berkshire Mountains in western

Fort Orange in 1639. Now under I-787.

Massachusetts, and from northwest Connecticut north to the Green Mountains in southern Vermont. They formed the great Mohican Confederacy and at the time numbered thousands.

It was the Mohicans that Henry Hudson met when he sailed up the river — named after him — in 1609, an event that proved fatal to the Mohicans. Disease brought on by contact with the Europeans, losses from war with the Mohawks to the West due to tensions over the fur trade, and broken promises by the Whites, decimated these people and forced them out of their homeland.

A group of Mohicans, then 'christianized,' left the area and founded Stockbridge (Mass.), but even here their days were numbered. After nearly loosing half the male population during the American Revolution (they sided with the colonists), the

Oneida Indians, who had also fought for the colonists, offered the "Stockbridge" people a portion of their land to live on in which they settled in the 1780s.

Again, this rich fertile land was taken by the Whites and the Mohicans migrated to the White River area in Indiana to live with their relatives, the Miami and Delaware. By the time they arrived the Delaware had already been cheated out their land.

Negotiations for a large tract of land in Wisconsin was initiated by the federal government, New York officials, and others, with the Menominee and Winnebago tribes, and the Mohicans began building a new village at Grand Cackalin called Statesburg. The treaty in 1822, allowed the Stockbridge and another group called the Munsee of the Delaware Confederacy in New Jersey to move, but the Menominee did not like the agreement and renegotiated. Finally the Mohicans and Munsee moved to two townships on the East shore of Lake Winnebago by 1834.

Another Treaty in 1856, saw the Stockbridge and Munsee move to the townships of Bartelme and Red Springs in Shawano County. The official name of the groups became the Stockbridge-Munsee Band of Mohican Indians.

The 1934 Indian Reorganization Act made it possible for the Stockbridge Munsee people to reorganize their tribal government and get back some of the land that had been lost by unscrupulous lumber dealers. About 15,000 acres of land in the township of Bartelme were purchased for the tribe.

Contrary to James Fennimore Cooper's, "The Last of the Mohicans," (read it at http://xtf.lib.virginia.edu/xtf/view?docId=2005_Q4_1/uvaBook/tei/eaf056v1.xml and http://xtf.lib.virginia.edu/xtf/view?docId=2005_Q4_1/uvaBook/tei/eaf056v2.xml) who in one stroke of the pen exterminated these people from the minds of the public, the Mohican Nation, Stockbridge-Munsee Band, are doing just fine today.

It is our contention that a living Mohican village be created in Albany, perhaps on the banks of the 'Muh-he-kun-ne-tuk' (where the waters were never still, or the river that flows both ways) — the Hudson River, at the Corning Preserve.

This living village would consist of several longhouses and would be utilized by members of the Mohican Nation as a living museum in which tourists could visit and learn the ways of a people that lived here in harmony with the land for thousands of

1697 view of Albany. Much of what you see is probably still underground waiting to be rediscovered.

years. Workshops and special events could take place seasonally. It would be the only living village of its kind in their original territorial limits.

The village would be tied into the overall Beverwyck Archeological Park.

**Making The Albany Plan Work**

In order to make the Albany Plan work, the leadership of this city should work together, not against, with organizations and interested citizens that specialize in local history and archeology; to promote the archeological park and to serve as a resource in locating, excavating, and promoting further archaeological resources, as well as standing historic structures in the city. A few notable organizations and projects with expertise are:

Capital District Preservation Task Force
Historic Albany Foundation
Albany County Historical Society (Ten Broeck Mansion)
Albany Institute of History and Art
New York State Museum and Science Service
Cherry Hill
Schuyler Mansion
Stockbridge-Munsee Band of the Mohican Indians
Colonial Albany Project

**City Museum of History and Archeology**

The city of Albany should establish an Albany City Museum to archive and display the prehistory and history collections that are obtained from the excavations of the Beverwyck Archeological Park, and other city excavations.

Albany had a museum starting in December 1797 on the corner of Green and Beaver Streets (known as the Vodde mart -"Rag Market"), later moving to City Hall (3rd floor), and later still moved to the Marble Column Building, on the NW corner of State and Broadway (known as the Johnny Robinson Corner from 1830-55) on December 1, 1830. The museum contained *"A number of living animals, and a great variety of other natural and artificial curiosities."* Light illumination by gas inside a building was first demonstrated here in March 22, 1817. The museum was discontinued on April 28, 1855.

In 1866, an Irish immigrant, Patrick McCarty, while excavating for a fire house, dug up parts of the stockade of the second line (between Hudson and Beaver Streets) of the defensive wall. He presented them to the Common Council and recommended the start of a new Albany Museum. No one knows where those posts are today.
In 1977, Don Rittner, then Albany City Archeologist, with a REAP Grant from the County of Albany began renovating the old St Paul's, later St. John's, Church on the corner of Dongan Avenue and South Ferry Street for use as a new Albany City Museum. However, this project was terminated with the refusal of the Catholic Diocese to turn over the building to the project after Rittner's group renovated the building. In 1978 this was going to be the Albany City Museum but after we put over $70,000 in restoring it the Diocese refused to give it to us.

Both New York City and Montreal have a city history museum that can be modeled after. The Pointe-à-Callière Museum in Montreal is the result of major archaeological

In 1978 this former church and school was going to be renovated into the Albany City Museum but after we put over $70,000 in restoring it the Catholic Diocese refused to give it to us.

discoveries on the site in the 1980s. John Wolcott took part in those excavations. The Museum is actually an integral part of the site. Rising above more than 1,000 years of human history, it houses and protects remarkable architectural remains, displayed in situ with respect for their integrity, along with hundreds of artifacts.

## Who do we target?

Who will visit the Beverwyck Archeological Park? It is obvious that local use and visitation by Capital District residents will be strong, as evidenced with the more than 1500 site seers that watched the excavations of the Albany Stockade behind the Federal Post Office Building in 1999.

However, Albany could promote this unique archeological park throughout the United States and beyond.

International visitors could be targeted from Canada, Holland, England, and Germany, in particular. Since New York City is a heavy tourist destination, heavy promotions in New York City hotels, entertainment, and travel institutions, would be viable since Albany is only a short train ride from the city.

The facts demonstrate that if Albany were to embrace its history rather than run away from it, the city would become a heritage destination for years to come — and that translates into millions of tourist dollars.

Today, it is clear that Albany does not receive visitors who want to gaze at the new office buildings or parking garages which stand on top of its history, and which represent architectural constipation in their design and structure. If Fort Orange, the original site of Albany, uncovered in 1968, had been turned into a museum instead of being buried by Interstate 787, the city would have gained millions of tourist dollars over this past 32 year period. Instead, millions of cars whiz by daily seeing Albany - like its great history — only as a blur.

Yes, this was written in 2000, the beginning of the new century. Can you imagine the tourist dollars flowing today if any of these suggestions were implemented?

Philip Schuyler's House on State and Pearl built in 1667 and torn down for a bank in 1924.

The city continued to knock down its Dutch history throughout the 20th century until there was not a single intact Dutch building left.

The **Pointe-à-Callière Museum** in Montreal, the museum of archaeology and history located in Old Montreal *"was founded in 1992 as part of celebrations to mark Montreal's 350th birthday. Set atop the city's birthplace, the Museum shows collections of artifacts from the First Nations of the Montreal region that illustrate how various cultures coexisted and interacted, and how the French and British regimes influenced the history of this territory over the years. Pointe-à-Callière has been recognized as a national historic site since 1998."*

Since it opened, it has seen more than 350,000 visitors a year. Nearly 4.5 million people have visited since 1992. Pointe-à-Callière has been honored with more than fifty national and international awards. If Albany had done something similar in 2000 when we first proposed this, what do you think the impact of tourism dollars would have been?

Clearly, preserving Albany's history means dollars and sense.

Pointe-à-Callière, Montreal. Here you can walk through ancient streets, look at building foundations and see thousands of artifact of the original Montreal. Why not Albany?

This Dutch house at 674 Broadway was torn down for no reason. The lot was vacant for years.

# Albany's History of Destroying its History

First published on February 1, 2014 4:37 pm

The last half of the 20th century and the first decade of this one have had deadly consequences on the historical and archeological resources of the city of Albany. During that time, the city has virtually wiped out its standing Dutch history and likewise has destroyed several key archeological sites in downtown.

Let's review it since the most important archeological site in the city may now be

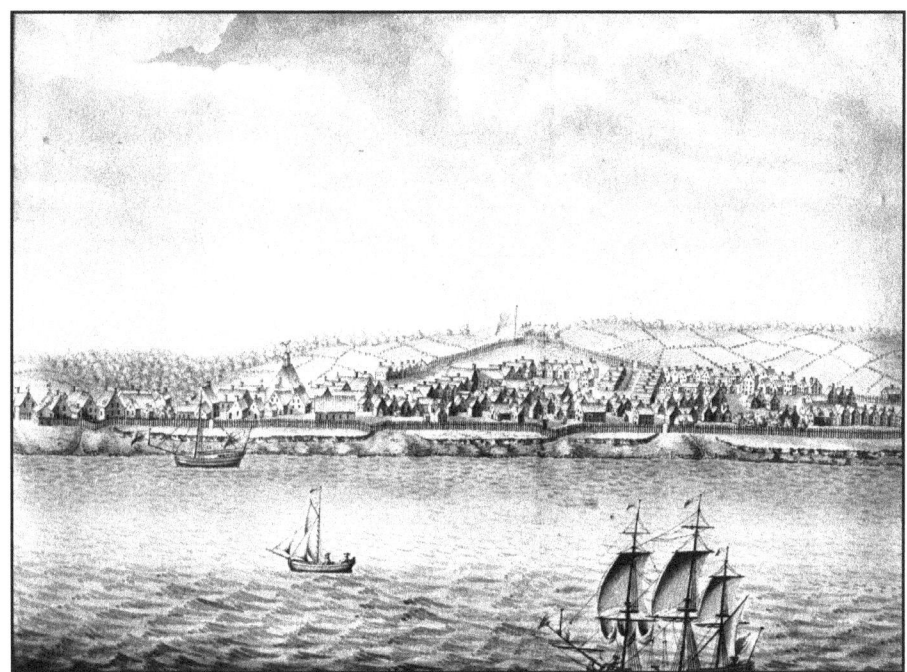

Albany in 1684 was full of Dutch architecture which has been removed one by one until any resemblance of Dutch culture is virtually non existent today.

threatened to go with the rest of them – Fort Nassau, the first Dutch settlement in the New World.

## 20th Century Removals

It is amazing that any of Albany's Dutch architecture survived into the 20th century given the long-term lack of interest by the city, but up to the 1950s there were several good examples still standing.

Widow Helen Sturdivant House on North Pearl Street. She moved in the house in 1820. Was a Dutch bakery before that. Was torn down when they built the extension of the Ten Eyck Hotel. Both are now gone.

James Eights painted North Pearl as he remembered in 1805 showing Widow Sturdivant's House.

## WIDOW STURDIVANT HOUSE, NORTH PEARL STREET

Helen Sturdivant moved in the house in 1820. This Dutch gabled home with fleur-de-lie wall ties was a Dutch bakery before that. It was torn down when they built the extension of the Ten Eyck Hotel. Both are now gone replaced with whatever that brick building is on the corner of State and North Pearl Street with no windows on the bottom floor.

## VANDENBURGH HOUSE, 674 BROADWAY

The Vandenburgh House was located at 674 Broadway between Clinton and Orange. The Federal Government thought it was important enough to photograph it and do detailed drawings by the Historic American Building Survey during the depression. The city shortly after had no problem with it being demolished.

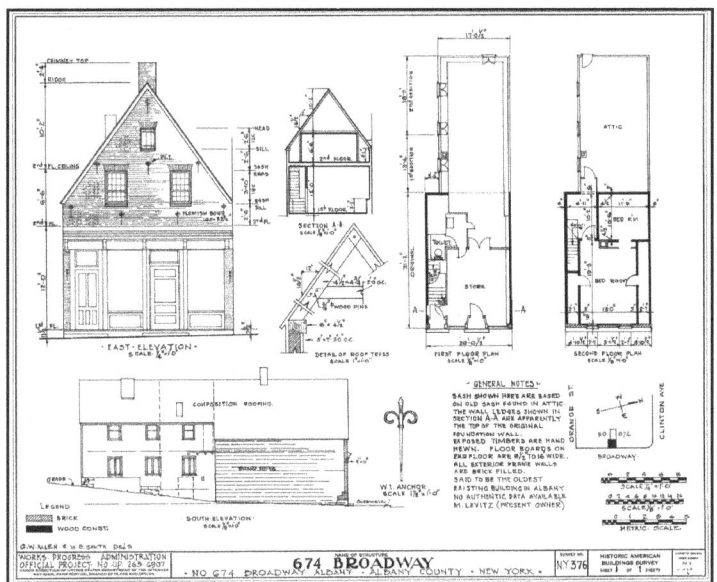
HABS Survey during the depression.

## 922 BROADWAY

This Dutch house built in 1734 was located between North Ferry and Thatcher and was also mapped by the HABS Project and shortly after it was demolished in 1934. It had an unusual shingle front.

The Vandenburgh House was demolished in the 1940s.

## WIDOW VISCHER HOUSE, COLUMBIA AND NORTH PEARL

This house was built by John Lansing, Revolutionary War officer. The celebrated house where Indians were in the habit of lodging on their visit to the city for the purpose of trading their furs. In 1749,

922 Broadway demolished in 1934.

Swedish Botanist Peter Kalm stayed here and described for the first time "Cole Slaw." Cole Slaw is Dutch for "Cabbage Salad." It was Pemberton's Store till 1886 when it was demolished during Albany's Bicentennial for Albany Business College.

JOHN SCHUYLER, JR. HOUSE, STATE AND SOUTH PEARL

Pemberton House on the corner of Columbia and North Pearl.

Southeast corner of State and Pearl. Home of John Schuyler, Jr. It was built by his father Philip Pietersen Schuyler, father of the first mayor of Albany in 1667. Torn down during the Albany's Bicentennial in 1886. Replaced by the Albany County Savings Bank. That's right I said during the city's Bicentennial right along with the Pemberton House.

Home of John Schuyler, Jr, built by his father Philip Pietersen Schuyler, father of the first mayor of Albany.

Fort Orange was partially excavated then covered by an Interstate ramp.

## ARCHEOLOGICAL SITES DEMOLISHED
## FORT ORANGE - 1624

Let's start with what probably was the first historic archeology dig in Albany in 1970-71. Local historian John Wolcott had discovered the location of Fort Orange, the second Dutch fort built after their first one, Fort Nassau, kept getting flooded out over on Castle Island (Port of Albany). Excavations were conducted by Paul Huey from the State but were rushed since the State was in a hurry to build a ramp over it for Interstate 787.

## SUNY CENTRAL GARAGE AND POST OFFICE - 1999

Stewart Dean had his house and docks here and in 1785 took his sloop *Experiment* across to China, the first such adventure ever. Yes, these were uncovered along with a 150 foot long section of the 1730 Albany Stockade, an 18th century dock, wharves, an Indian site, and a mid 17th century fire pit mixed with Indian and European goods below it. If they had given up a few parking spots you could be admiring it today.

## NYS DORMITORY AUTHORITY - 1996

East of Broadway between Maiden Lane and Steuben Street. This was an entire block of the original Beverwyck covered by the new building. Found was the house site of Mayor Abraham Yates built in 1662. Next to it was the Dutch Minister's house. The archeology was

Fort Orange today.

The oldest rum distillery in America covered by a parking garage.

rushed on this site and there should have been more time allowed for proper examination. A great deal of Dutch artifacts were recovered.

DEC BUILDING 625 BROADWAY 1998

Just outside the original north gate of the city. Foundations were found of colonial buildings before the big fire of 1792. A Native American site was found as well. The Department of Environmental Conservation occupies the site now.

THE ALBANY RUM DISTILLERY - 2001

What do you do when you find the oldest rum distillery in North America? Why you bury it so you can put a six-story parking lot on it. That's what happened in 2001. This is what the newspaper said: *"Perhaps the 4,000 visitors who crammed the distillery site before last week's burial, packing restaurants and clearing gift shop shelves at the nearby Albany Visitors Center, convinced Jennings that it might be worthwhile to make more of his city's 400-year history, especially in light of his efforts to revitalize the downtown. But he said this had always been his intention."*

*"It's not a change of heart on my part,"* he said. *"We've undergone a billion dollars worth of growth and development in the last six years and for a city that was dormant for so long, we had to prioritize."*

The 60 x 36 foot distillery was built in 1758-59 and contained 18-21 vats with interconnected wooden pipes, a still, fireplace, privy and foundation of the manager's house. Anywhere else

The Rum Distillery is now under this garage.

30

Key Bank.

this would have been preserved. Not so in one of the oldest cities in America. Thanks to donations from a couple of local businessman two of the vats were recovered and preserved and now you can see them at the State Museum, totally out of context of course.

Part of this dig uncovered a brick makers house that contained the earliest archeological evidence of a jamless fireplace. If they moved the footprint of the parking garage a few feet they could have saved the entire distillery site.

Here are more photos: http://www.donrittner.com/albanydig.html

KEY BANK ALMS HOUSE, SOUTH PEARL

Another celebration with destruction during the city's 1986 Tercentennial Celebration took place half way between Pearl Street and Green Street. Omni Development was building the Key Bank building. Excavations revealed the 1647 house of Volkert Jansen Douw, a wealthy trader and land speculator and is earlier than the

Another estruction of history next to the former post office.

Brick with hand print recovered from the Mayor Yates house site by historian John Wolcott.

establishment of Beverwyck. After his death the house was remodeled in 1685 by the Dutch Reformed Church of Albany and became the city's new almshouse, owned and operated by the Reformed Church. Part of this site also revealed an Indian Mission Church. The site basically became a mint, making wampum for the Native trade. Burials were found south of this site that may have been related to the original Dutch Reformed Church burial ground of the 17th century.

WHAT COULD HAVE BEEN?

Instead of a sterile downtown Albany of modern buildings and parking garages we could be benefiting from millions in tourist dollars if the archeological sites had been incorporated into the design of each of these projects. Thousands of heritage tourists would have been flocking to see the only place in the country that would have had this assemblage of 17th century Dutch history.

Why this did not happen can probably be summed up by a young girl from the Female Academy in Albany who wrote this in 1845.

Dormitory Authority building takes up a whole block of the original Beverwyck.

32

DEC Building.

*"Albany, city of my birth! Ancient, yet new! Replete with interesting associations of the past, connected by so many links with the present, and promising to posterity a glorious future. They antique dwellings have been leveled, not so much by the hand of Time, as the merciless spirit of improvement.*

*Goths and Vandals! Ye were the sweet dispensers of the charities of life, compared to the demon who now stalks abroad under that abused name.*

*Where now are the palaces of the Knickerbockers and the Van Winkles? Gone! Leveled with the dust, or oh! Worse, far worse, modernized!*
*Why the very Holland bricks — if they could speak, would cry shame! And the substantial beams fall down and crush the walls in their deep despair, when they are subjected to the degrading process of modernizing!*

*Shades of our fathers! Why is it permitted? To renovate, to preserve those remnants of the past, should be our pious aim, not with profane hands to cut, hew down, and alter the roof trees which have sheltered generation after generation."*
———**The Monthly Rose, Albany Female Academy, 1845**

If a young girl over a century ago understood the city's history and significance, why can't the rest of the population get it today?

If you would like a few more ideas of what we can do with our buried treasure read the following:

The Albany Historium
The Albany Plan of Preservation
Such Promise But No Vision

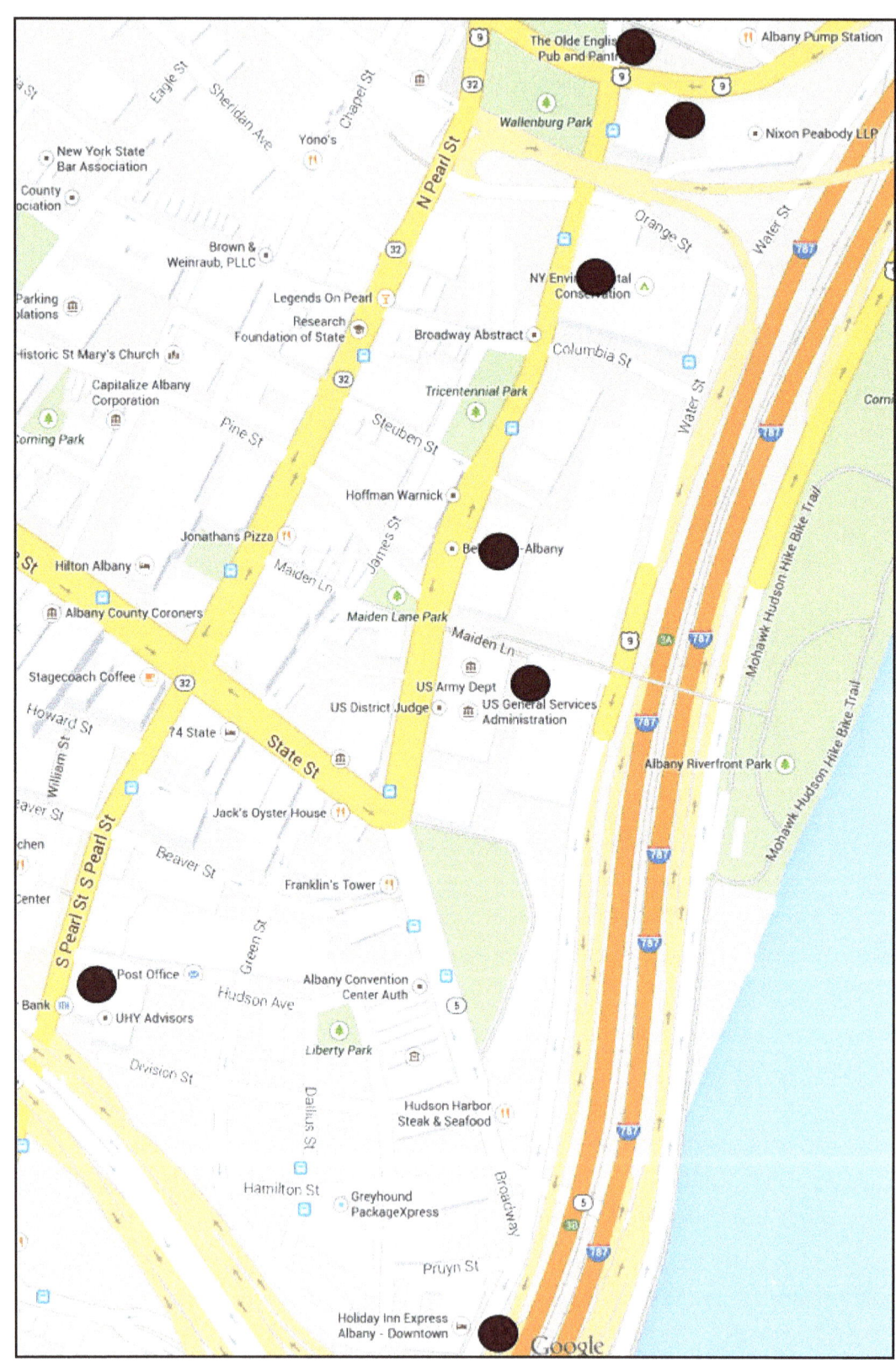

Location of sites covered over. This could have been a 17th century walking tour of Albany.

# Don't Judge a Book by its Cover (or a building by its facade)!
First published on September 13, 2016 1:58 pm

In old cities like Troy, Albany, or Schenectady that are two hundred years or older, it is not uncommon to find buildings that have withstood the test of time. They are often refurbished and altered over the years so by present standards it is hard to recognize their real age or significance architecturally. Many have what I call "garbage facades" slapped over them to hide the "old" original facades.

This happens often when a residential building is turned into a commercial or retail establishment. Often the first floor facade is ripped out and some gaudy replacement is built.

A good example are numbers 48 and 50 Hudson Avenue in Albany that made the news recently. Number 50, a Federal period home built around 1810 by Ira Jenkins, but covered over and altered, was razed because of Albany's continued policy of "demolition by neglect," and the State's Convention Center office, which owned it, ignoring the needs of the building.

Number 50 has a colorful history. A web page on the genealogy of the family of Richard Perry Radcliff was looking for a relative named Minni W. Shannon (http://rpradcliffe.com/887.htm) and came up with some interesting information on this building. This is what the page says:

"*Information about 50 Hudson Ave: The address of 50 Hudson was, in 1878, owned by a temperance group, and had a reading room. On Mar. 27, 1890 -- Carrie Parshall was in court because her gold watch had been stolen and Ira Brackett was arrested for it. Carrie was living at this address.*

*On Oct. 26, 1893, the paper mentions a birthday party for a nine-year-old named Carrie Bauerlein at this address.*

*On Oct. 9, 1894, the Morning Express has an article about Charles D. Rathbone having his place of business at this address. He was a seller of leather, and there was a case against him. In 1868 he formed a partnership with Isaac Lefevre under the name of Rathbone & Lefevre*

*Charles Wait and Carrie Parscall were both at 50 Hudson in 1894.*"

For many Albanians, Number 50 was the home of Capital City Rescue Mission until recently.

Numbers 48 and 50 Hudson in 1931. Number 48 was an equipment retail store and 50 was the TallyHo bar. From this photo you would never know there was one of Albany's last Dutch houses surviving behind the garbage facade. Personal collection.

On Jan. 23, 1896, this article was front and center of the Albany Morning Express, page one:

*"Rena Cried Murder. When Hattie had Pulled Up a Large Lock of Her Hair by the Roots - Then the Police Came. At an early hour this morning the police were startled by the cries of murder in the vicinity of Hudson Avenue and Green Street. Upon investigation it was found that Rena Moore and Hattie E. Wendell, occupying portions of the house No. 50 Hudson avenue, was indulging in a fracas and that Hattie had succeeded in pulling a large handful of hair from Rena's head. But for the timely arrival of Sargent Cuddy and Officers Hoffman and Wilson, the Moore woman would probably have been scalped. It seems that the Moore woman rents the entire house from an agent and sublets a portion to the Wendell woman. For many years No. 50 Hudson Avenue has been known as a disorderly house and disturbances have been frequent. Hattie Wendell is but 18. She was arrested for a breach of the peace and Rena Moore, aged 26, was taken for a breach of the peace and keeping a disorderly house."*

The next day, the follow-up article was:

*"Rena Moore and Hattie Wendell arrested early yesterday morning for creating a breach of the peace at No. 50 Hudson avenue, were fined five dollars each in Police court yesterday morning."*

The year after Minnie died (1895), someone died in the building of natural causes and was buried in Potter's field.

At this address on Nov. 28, 1895, as printed in the next day's Times-Union:

*"Free for all Fight. One of the Participants Stabbed -- The Examination in Court. There was a birthday party at Josey Cramer's, No. 50*

Another View of 48 Hudson, c 1873. Courtesy John Ham.

*Hudson Avenue, last evening. Among those who called to wish the hostess long life and happiness were B. Anthony Evans, aged 31 years, married and ... John Lyons, John Lyman and Theodore Cramer, Josey's brother-in-law. Two of Josey's boarders Irene Hadley and Rena Moore, were also present. A turkey dinner had been prepared and a keg of beer was placed in the kitchen to drown the bird. As the lager was free, all the guests insisted on drinking many times and the keg soon ran dry, but the participants in the feast were mellow and hilarious. Suddenly there was a free for all fight and dishes, chairs and fists were flying through the air. Lyman struck Evans, and Cramer who came to his assistance, was hit in the eye and went down. He picked himself up and made his exit. Evans received a knife*

Number 48 Hudson Street. George Stoneman occupied the house from 1892-1923 but still owned it in 1926. Courtesy of John Ham.

This is 48 and 50 Hudson shortly before 48 was donated to the Historic Albany Foundation. Number 50 was torn down shortly after.

*thrust in the left leg and accused Lyman of the act. After the participants had separated Evans, who was very intoxicated, was assisted to a near-by saloon where Dr. Colbert dressed his wounds. Sergeant Becket with Patrolmen ... visited the house and took in custody Josey, Theodore and Lyons. At the station house Evans insisted that Lyman did the cutting. Lyman, Irene and Rena escaped from the house before the police made the raid...."*

Also in 1897(?) (Same year as Josey's party) is this article from the Albany Morning Express:

*"James Boyle, 24 years old, was arrested by Officers Lawton and Gorman, late last night, charged with an assault on Grace McAuley, of No. 50 Hudson avenue. The woman claimed that Boyle came into the house and after abusing her kicked her in the stomach."*

Late 19th century photo showing 48 Hudson before the facade was changed.

In March 1899, a traveling salesman apparently living here hanged himself in a kitchen.

In the 1930s and '40s, it was a tavern, the *"Tally-Ho,"* with the *"hottest floor show in town"* according to the Albany Times Union. It was a rescue mission for many years, including 1969.

Number 48 Hudson, built in 1728, and perhaps the oldest building in Albany, is known as the Van Ostrand House and probably is the last remaining Dutch building located within the confines of the walled in village during the 18th century. (Contrary to what you heard on TV or read in the paper, the house was located WITHIN the Stockade not outside it). It was Albany historian John Wolcott who brought the public's attention to this building back in 1989 to the Historic Resources Commission!

Henry Coughtry had bought it from Samuel Norton in 1822. Coughtry sold it to an Issac Holt in 1833 who in turn sold it to Jared Holt in 1835. Holt was there as early as 1828. He had a fire in the store in 1836. Loss was 15k, it was 18 below zero temperature. In 1871 it was Jared and CB Holt and Dayton Ball. In 1890, it was Dayton Ball & Co making hats, taking over from the Holt family. In 1916 there was

> LEATHER AND FINDINGS—The subscriber continues to keep on hand at his Leather and Finding Store, 48 Hudson street, Albany, a superior assortment of Stock and Tools for Boot and Shoemakers' use which he will sell at wholesale and retail at the lowest prices for cash or approved credit.
> Shoe Manufacturers, Merchants, Pedlars, and all who use or deal in the above articles, are respectfully invited to call and examine his stock before purchasing elsewhere. He offers a good assortment of Oak and Hemlock Sole and Upper Leather, French and American Calf Skins, Kips, Splits, &c., a superior assortment of Morocco, and of excellent quality, Linings and Roans of all colors, Bindings, &c., Prunelle, Satin Francis, Galloons, Ribbons, Silk and Cotton Laces, Boot Web, Cord, &c. Lasts and Boot Trees, Shoe Threads of all numbers, Shoe Nails, Pegs Hammers, Pinchers, Awls, Rasps, Tacks Patent Handles, Kit and Shoe Tools, and Findings of every description.
> N. B. All who send orders may depend on receiving articles of as good quality and as cheap as if they were present to select for themselves.
> oc11      JARED HOLT 48 Hudson street.

Holt's advertisement for his services in a 19th century Albany City Directory.

the Jared Hold Co, shoe makers. They were making stitching wax still in 1918, was still around in 1951.

Between 1931 and 1938 this classic Dutch house disappeared as a new ugly facade was attached to it. Fortunately much of the original fabric, the East pitched roof, east wall, and structural members are still intact which will help in the restoration if it happens.

It was owned by a private person recently who was going to restore it but gave up and donated it to Historic Albany Foundation (HAF).

HAF, while dismal in keeping buildings up over the last few years, (though not for lack of trying), conducted a survey a while ago of all the buildings standing that were built before the Civil War. Assuming the City of Albany received this information in some form, a lack of action in securing, or at least assessing the conditions of each of them, shows a complete lack of interest in preserving its history. Yes, there was a lot

---

**JARED HOLT,**

# LEATHER AND FINDING STORE,

### No. 48 HUDSON STREET,

Between Green and Union Street,

## ALBANY, N. Y.

Constantly on hand Oak and Hemlock Sole Leather, French and American Calf Skins, Linings, Bindings, Morocco, Lasts, and Boot Trees; Shoe Maker's Tools and Findings of all kinds. Best Oak Tanned Belting; Lace and String Leather, at wholesale and retail, at the lowest market price.

Holt's advertisement for his services in a 19th century Albany City Directory.

After Historic Albany Foundation obtained the building they cleverly put up a mockup of the original facade. The non profit organization is now restoring it for their offices.

of talk about how important it was when the new administration came in, but as they say, talk is cheap. There has been no movement on putting in any safeguards for protection (as seen by the demolition of Number 50 and several others that were on the survey list) and the city's Historic Sites Commission seems paralyzed.

## Holy Innocents Church

The Albany Historic Sites Commission is going to decide on October 5 at 5:30PM at Albany City Hall, Council Chambers (You should show up and make your voice heard to save the church) on whether Hope House can tear down Holy Innocents Church in the Arbor Hill neighborhood, one of the most important architectural landmarks that you will hear about shortly. The church was put on the National Register of Historic Places back in 1978. Hope House is pleading economic hardship for tearing it down. They have owned it since 1997 so what is their excuse for not doing something for the last twenty years? Again John Wolcott called public attention to this church in 2003 to a city's deaf ear. There is a newsreel sitting on the shelves of Time Warner's then-named News Channel 9 where reporter Elizabeth Hur interviewed Wolcott talking about the importance of this building in April 2003. On April 14, 2003, Wolcott was interviewed by Times Union reporter Brian Nearing when he introduced an application to the city's Historic Resource Commission to extend a nearby local historic district to include the church. At the time, the city's historic preservation planner Richard Nicholson said, *"this is the first request from a citizen to extend a district since the first districts were created in 1988, after the city created its historic resources law."* Historic Albany Foundation supported the measure. Yes, that is thirteen years ago. Albany has the dubious distinction of being the "Demolition Capital of America" according to Wolcott. Historic Albany Foundation named the church one of the city's most endangered historic assets over a decade ago. The irony of all of this is a March 17, 2000 Times Union article titled "Albany retains its historic character - Commission has

Holy Innocents drawing from Munsell's Collection.

Holy Innocents now. Courtesy of John Wolcott.

Holy Innocents has been deteriorated for years. Photo by Don Rittner.

been keeping its eye on 3,500 buildings in designated districts," starts off with this opening paragraph: *"Month after month, year after year, the city's Historic Resources Commission has been keeping its eye on the 3,500 buildings in designated historic districts, most of which are located in center city neighborhoods."* Count the number of buildings that have come down in Albany since 2000.

According to the application to demolish the church by HH Funding Corp (Hope House or Howard Hubbard?), the application cites that a demolition permit is being sought because the building "is not capable of earning a reasonable return" by the current owner or any other potential buyer, and thus should be demolished. However according to a recent Times Union article Hope House is trying to solidify plans with a "a new owner who will rehabilitate the building before then." According to Kevin Connally, Executive Director, he is quoted as *"absolutely we're trying to save it."* Huh? He goes on to say, *"The goal is to find a suitable buyer that has the resources to stabilize it and do something productive with it, that doesn't hinder the community. There are two parties interested in purchasing the church, and preserving it in some capacity,"* Connally basically contradicting his own demolition permit request? Then why are they trying to demolish it? The city requested that they get a demolition permit for 102 Colonie Street, the parsonage behind the church.

According to Wolcott, Holly Innocents was designed by architect Frank Wills, in 1850, based on his earlier Gothic Revival designed St Anne's Chapel of Ease, in Fredericton, New Brunswick, built in 1846-47.

Wills wrote the book on American Gothic Revival; a real book, "Ancient English Ecclesiastical Architecture," in 1850. Both Holy Innocents and Grace Church, both his designs, are illustrated. Grace Church is gone so Holy Innocents is the last remaining Wills church in Albany.

You can download your own copy of his book here:

St. Anne's Chapel of Ease, Fredericton, New Brunswick, the blueprint for Holy Innocents. Designed by Frank Wills.

https://books.google.com/books/about/Ancient_English_ecclesiastical_architect.html?id=BZIZAAAAYAAJ

Holy Innocents has stained glass windows designed by the Bolton Brothers (in particular John Bolton, brother of William Jay). One window is smashed. John was known for skillfully painting texts and probably painted the Te Deum all around the nave walls in Holy Innocents according to Wolcott. The opening double line beautifully lettered TE Deum Laudamus is completely smashed. John Bolton is famous for some masterful and extremely unique historically lettering in Christ Church, Pelham, he added. Pelham is where the two brothers produced the first figurative stained glass ever in the US and it was the Gift of The Magi as the East window over the altar. Needless to say the windows in Holy Innocents have some significance.

A good overview of the issue can be read here written by Paula Lemire calling for its preservation back in May, 2015 when a section of it collapsed:

http://albanynyhistory.blogspot.com/2015/05/seriously-endangered-church-of-holy.html

Holy Innocents in better days. Courtesy John Wolcott.

Here is another:

http://albanyruralcemetery.blogspot.com/2015/05/the-dewitt-children-and-church-of-holy.html

The deterioration of this church is squarely to blame on the city of Albany, Hope House, and former Bishop Howard Hubbard who founded it and controls its funding operation according to Wolcott. When part of the church collapsed the Times Union reported that Historic Albany Foundation was working with Hope House and Albany Housing Authority along with the city in looking at ways to stabilize it. Nothing came of it and the church continued to deteriorate. We shall await the fate of this church on October 5th.

This nonsense is not confined to Albany. Troy and Schenectady are just as bad. Schenectady (Metroplex) recently tore down several early 19th century buildings on lower State Street, not even blinking an eye that they were just as important as the city's Historic Stockade. They represented some of the earliest structures outside the original stockade village, which also suffers from neglect. In the process of tearing down State Street an important later 19th century landmark on the corner of State and Erie Blvd was damaged and will be torn down later (not yet) as a result. Lawsuits have been filed. It reminded me of the Keystone Cops.

A really good example of my argument is Number 9 Front Street in Schenectady. A walk by this stucco two-story house looks like any basic 19th century building. Nothing spectacular to look at but beneath that stucco is

Number 9 Front Street looks like a typical 19th century home today. Photo by Don Rittner.

something else. It always bothered me when I walked past it because it was an odd shape for a house, not a rectangle house plan, but a square building. Houses are generally not built square. A small opening between it and the abutting building revealed the wall was built with flagstone with no windows. After further research and a crawl through the attic, I was able to determine it originally was a French and War era

Attic of 9 Front Street showing that all walls were flagstone. Photo by Don Rittner.

Blockhouse that was converted to a house after the fire of 1819 which burned down much of Schenectady's early business community. I was fortunate enough to have tree ring dating on the basement timbers and attic that proved my theory. The PBS show "History Detectives" did an episode about my findings in 2008 (http://www.pbs.org/opb/historydetectives/investigation/front-street-blockhouse/).

Demolition by neglect was also pretty common in Troy until recently. Part of the slow down is the immigration of young people and entrepreneurs that see the beauty in these old buildings and have been restoring them. Some notable examples are the old Quackenbush Department Store on the corner of Broadway and Third, the former Brown Hotel on Broadway near Second, the former Trojan Hardware Building on Congress, and former horse stable (now Innovation Garage) on Fourth Street.

I recently discovered two River Street buildings that are also good examples of my "don't judge" theory. During Troy's early days in the 18th and 19th centuries, the river was the landing place for ships loaded with cargo that was then carried up through the back of the River Street stores to the retail space fronting River Street. After Front Street was created; a service road near the river, it allowed wagons and later trolleys and trains to perform the same function. As Troy grew, so did the buildings on River Street. Some were replaced, some burned, some had another floor added or an extension was built in the back.

Numbers 210 (two-story) and 212 (three-story) have an interesting story to tell. Originally known as 212 and 212 ½ (originally there was a separating wall in the

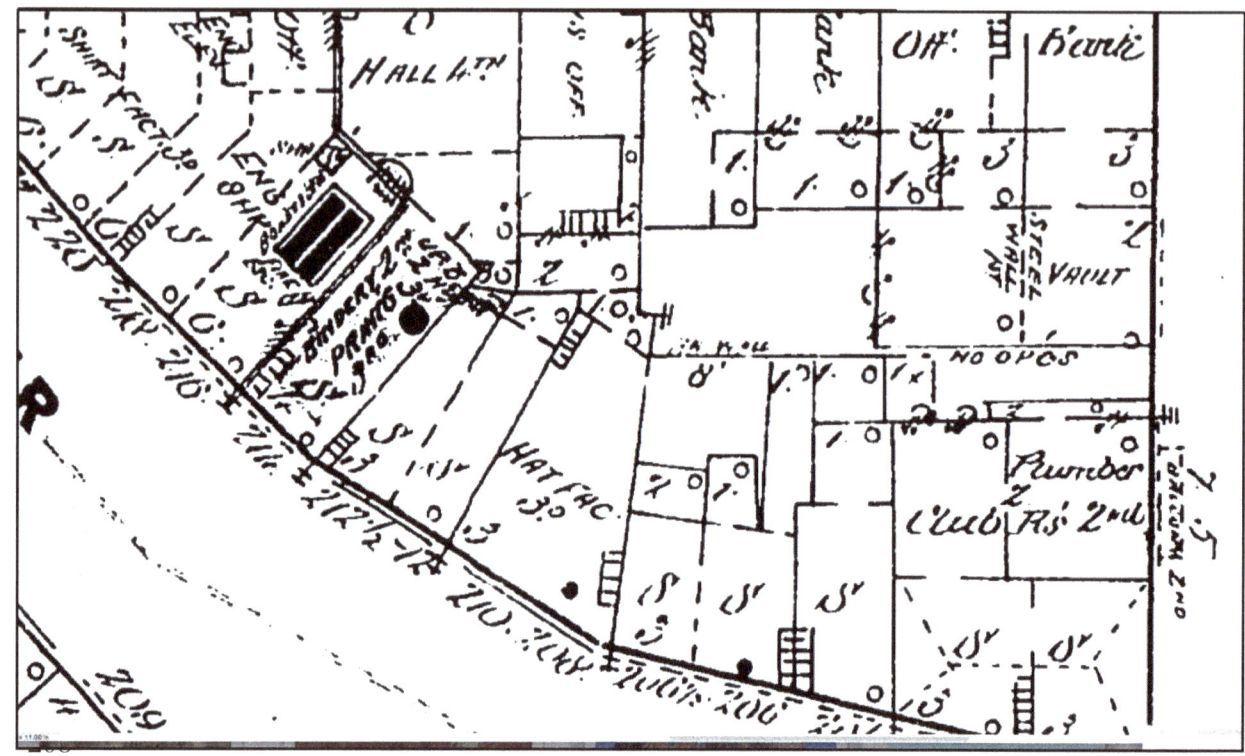

The 1885 Sanborn Insurance map showing both buildings were originally 3 story.

building creating two stores), and 208-210 (now just 210) these two buildings have a similar looking facade but they are not original. Number 210 has a date stone on the top left of 1845 and in the middle a date of 1870 and on the right 1884.

Both buildings may be renovated buildings from after the disastrous 1820 fire that burned most of the area within Congress and First

210 and 212 River from Google View. Today the buildings are still be occupied. Google Maps.

48

Streets and to the River. It was stopped at number 225 River. This is what was reported in the paper about the buildings burned on the East side:

*"Proceeding up River street on the east side, beginning at H. & Vail's brick stores, opposite the Post-office. Mr., McGready, three two-story wood buildings, occupied by James Adams as a shoe store, and D. McKelsie as a chair factory and sales shop, and Miss Brown, milliner. P. Heartt & Sons, one-story wood office, occupied by Wm. M. Bliss, Esq. P. Heartt & Sons, three-story brick front, occupied by James Wallace as a grocery and dwelling, and three other families for dwellings. P. Heartt & Sons, three-story elegant brick store, filled with hardware from the cellar to the garret Nathan Betts, two-story wood, occupied by Mr. Hicks as a grocery and dwelling. C. Adriance, two-story wood, occupied by Mr. Taylor and Mr. Deming. George Tibbits, three-story brick front, occupied by two widows as groceries and dwellings. C. Pease, two-story wood, occupied by Thomas Houghton, grocer. Seven two-story wood, five owned by Benjamin Covell, one by J. Weld, one owner unknown, occupied by Mr Defreest as a grocery, provision store and dwelling. Mr. Douglass, saddler's shop and dwelling. Wm, Osborne, bakery and dwelling. Mr. Hascall, millinery shop and dwelling. Weld & Brandt, coppersmith's shop and stove factory William Perry, locksmith. George White, printer, dwelling house. E. Reed, shoemaker's shop and dwelling. Jesse Boutwell, Miss Wilson, and probably other dwellings.*

*"D. G. Bears, two-story wood, stables, horse shed and a one-story house adjoining, occupied by Amos Allen as a tavern, north-east corner of State and River streets. Moore & Pitcher, two-story brick store and dwelling. Joseph Brintnall, two-story wood, dry goods. Warren & Co., three-story brick, occupied by Southwick, Cannon & Warren, wholesale dry goods. Hart & Nazro, hardware. D. Lane, dry goods. I. M. Wells, druggist, the books, papers, &c., about $100 in cash, belonging to the County medical society, are lost , Troy library, best part, some cash and some account books. Pierce & Sacket, crockery. M. McFadden, dry goods and millinery. William S. Parker, book store, bindery and office of the Troy Post; all three story brick, and owned by A. & D. Lane, (now Hall's building)."*

Number 225 River Street has an inscription on stopping the fire carved

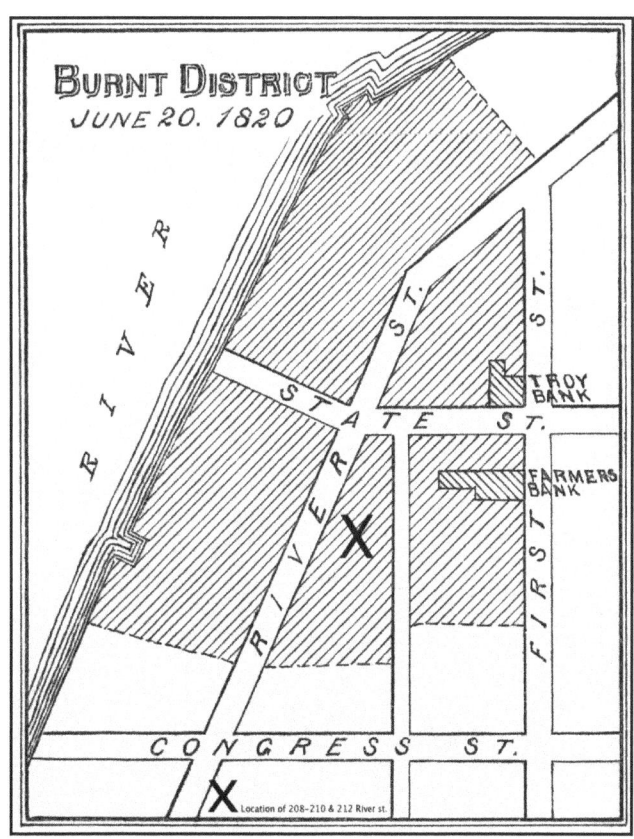

X marks the location of 208-210 and 212 River Street during the 1820 fire.

49

into its sandstone front.

Whether 210 and 212 were completely burned and then built from the ground up I am not sure but the date of 1845 on No. 210 suggests a beginning date for the business that was there since we know it was occupied previously (and after the fire of 1820). Since both facades are similar in design, 210 could have "borrowed" from 212 or both buildings had new similar fronts put on.

We also know that two additions were added in the back of 210, the last one probably in 1856 because that date, along with other initials, are carved in the bricks.

In 1837, R. D. & D. McMurray operated their real estate office at 210 River Street. In 1838 number 210 was the Troy Brush Factory also advertised by R. D. ad D. McMurray. In 1843, William A. McLauchlan's New One Price Cash Store occupied 210. In 1852 J. C. Mattice had his Boston Clothing Hall there. In 1854 the Troy Times moved into the building at 208 River and stayed until 1862. They probably added the extension in the back that has the 1856 date on the brick. In 1865 Johnson & Barrett's clothing store occupied 208-210.

See my article on initial carving "Leaving Your Mark."

The date 1856 carved in the stone is located on the back most addition on 210 and was probably added by the Troy Press. Photo by Don Rittner.

On January 26, 1867, a fire broke out at 210 River on Saturday at 10PM. It was occupied by J. Carnell, tailor and Wilson. The building next door (212) was badly damaged by water. It was occupied by Charles Vandecker, Dr. Irwin, Dentist, and W. F. Boshart, publisher of the Sunday Herald. It was declared arson. Could this be when the new facades were put on number 210 to mimic 212 that only suffered water damage? Or perhaps both had the new facades placed?

In 1869, 210 was the offices of the Troy Daily Press. Also in 1869, a new newspaper was published at 208-210, The Polytechnic, a semi monthly of twelve pages. The prospectus said it was to establish the paper permanently as a high-class college scientific publication and was connected to RPI. The Polytechnic is still RPI's student newspaper but they are advertising an 1885 beginning date. Sorry kids, you are older. In 1870 it was the printing press of Parmenter & Clark.

Troy, NY scratched incised. In case someone didn't know?

In 1878, the building was the Job and Printing House of the Troy Daily Press and by 1880-1882 the Troy Observer (circulation 2500). In 1892 Joseph P. Dugan made and sold fine hats and furs from then

This appears to spell out "Peters" which could be a brick employee. This wall would not have been visible to the public since another building was adjacent to it. Photo by Don Rittner.

208 & 210 River Street. In 1895 this is what "The Industries of Troy" wrote about the firm:

*P. DUGAN,*
*Hatter and Furrier, 208 and 210 River Street.*

*This important and leading house was established in 1872, and soon became the chief source of supply for fine headwear for gentlemen, and each year has added to its reputation and trade in all kinds of ladies' and gentlemen's furs and fur garments. The premises occupied for the business embrace a commodious three-story building, the ground floor forming a large double store-room, which is elegantly and attractively appointed with hard-wood fixtures and show cases, and a superb plate glass front that is one of the chief features of the principal business thoroughfare of the city. Mr. Dugan is sole agent in this city for the celebrated "Knox" silk and soft hats and derbys, which are widely recognized as the best hats manufactured in America. In furs and fur garments the stock includes fine seal sacques, jackets, capes, etc., and fur coats, cloaks and other garments. He is a practical furrier and an expert judge of all kinds of furs, and makes a specialty of making seal garments for ladies to order, his products in this direction being unsurpassed for high quality of material, style, fit and finish, and far superior to the ready-made fur garments usually offered to customers. Mr. Dugan is an enterprising business man closely identified with the progress of Troy, and his establishment is an honorable and successful factor of the trade accommodations of this city.*

Dugan eventually took over 208, 210, 212, and 214 River Streets by 1913. It was the Sanderson Paper Company in 1917, E. R. Robinson Book Store in 1920, and it has been the offices for TAP for a number of years now. As you can see there have been a number of business uses for the building.

There is evidence that both buildings may in fact be older. Number 212 has Dutch derived

One of the bricks had a kitten paw impression made while the bricks were still wet before baking. It is common to find animal marks, initials and even hand prints on pre-baked bricks. Photo by Don Rittner. Are these "Uncle Sam" Wilson's bricks?

wall ties holding the beams to the brick walls. You can see these on the North wall of the building where a former building stood (number 214). Walls ties are great dating tools since they hold the floor beams to the walls they are usually not removed and there is a rough dating method to them based on the way they are made and shaped.

You can also see the outline of the original peaked roof, which has been filled in on the sides to make it rectangular, a common method of the time. This is probably when the new facade was put on as well. I would guess this building really dates to the late 18th or early 19th century.

Looks like F.S.H.? Photo by Don Rittner.

This building had an interesting tenant in the 19th century, William H. Farnham, a banjo maker. Originally from Pennsylvania he set up shop here and worked from 1866 to 1875 (some same 1890). He fashioned banjos in odd designs constantly experimenting while most of his necks were made without a perch pole being bolted directly to the hoop. He also made banjos with the wooden hoop veneered with German silver, a style he picked up from the banjo maker that he succeeded, "the

Who knows who "H" is. Photo by Don Rittner

Several Dutch derived wall ties hold the floor beams to the brick walls on number 212 River St. Photo by Don Rittner.

Closeup of Dutch derived style wall tie. Photo by Don Rittner.

Original building of 212 River Street (black lines) with location of dutch derived style wall ties (arrows). North wall. Photo by Don

Close up of bent Dutch derived style wall tie on 212 River. Photo by Don Rittner.

Number 212 today. Photo by Don Rittner.

character" Albert Wilson, the son of "Uncle Sam" Wilson. Albert lived with at his father's place at 77 Ferry Street. He was a silversmith by trade but experimented in making banjos and drums. He exhibited both at the Union Fair in 1865 on Island Park. Union Fair was a combined Albany and Rensselaer County fair.

Wilson was making silver items as early as 1834 and died on July 22, 1866. Farnham picked up from there. This is

Number 210 today. Notice the window treatments are the same as number 212. Photo by Don Rittner.

what the Vintage Banjo Maker says about Wilson:

*"A banjo maker of Troy, New York, was called by S. S. Stewart "an eccentric genius" who was "much liked by players of his day." About the year 1850 he constructed a banjo which had a solid iron hoop and thirty iron brackets fitted with*

Y wall tie on 210 River, north wall. Could this be William Young who published many histories of Troy? Photo by Don Rittner.

Additions to Number 210 River. The inscribed bricks are on the last wall to the right. Photo by Don Rittner. There are two wall anchors to the top left on 210 River that are in the form of an "I"

*elaborate thumb screws for tightening the vellum. It proved too heavy for practical use apart from it being crudely made. The neck was merely bolted to the hoop and the instrument could not be relied upon to keep in tune.*

*About twenty years later he made a much lighter banjo which known as the "Sliver Rim" banjo and established a pattern for the majority of banjo makers. This instrument had a wooden hoop veneered with thin German silver (white brass) that was rolled over the top and bottom edges of the hoop.*

*Wilson became adept at the use of German silver, making ingenious articles using it, which he sold."*

Obvious it wasn't twenty years later since Wilson died in 1866 so it was earlier. Vintage Banjo Maker also wrote:

*"Although his eccentricity caused him to fashion banjos in many odd designs by way of experiment, he finally adhered to the legitimate instrument and was deemed to be the best banjo maker of his time. Many of his instruments for professionals were profusely inlaid with mother of pearl, silver and fancy woods."*

*"His successor, William H. Farnham, continued to make the Wilson banjo up until the 1890s without any appreciable modifications."*

Another merchant who was at 212 River was Anthony Lawton, Clothes dealer and merchant Taylor in 1871. David E. Alman received a patent at that address in 1997 for PROCESS FOR PRODUCING FINELY DIVIDED INTERMETALLIC AND CERAMIC POWDERS AND PRODUCTS THEREOF.

So the next time you look at an old building remember that it probably has more history than you will ever have.

Furthermore this policy of demolition by neglect in the Capital District needs to stop. However, unless you hold your elected officials to the fire it will continue as usual and more and more of our local urban history will be gone and replaced by empty lots, vanilla boxes, and a sense of visual homogenization.

The uncovered portion of the Albany Stockade in the early 2000s only to be buried again with a building placed on top of it.

# What Do You Do When You Find The Roots Of Your Historic City?

First published on January 27, 2014 2:10 pm

If you are Montreal, Canada, you excavate carefully then build a museum around it that attracts thousands to your city each year.

If you are Albany, you might allow the building of a crude oil boiling facility on top of it. That is the choice facing Albany right now.

When Montreal archeologists located the original birthplace of their city in the 1980s, they spent the next decade carefully excavating the site. Not only did it represent the history of Montreal's founding but also over 1000 years of Native occupation before that. They uncovered buildings, streets, defensive walls, and thousands of artifacts and built a museum over the site that opened in 1992.

Today Pointe-à-Callière, a recognized national historical and archaeological site, leads visitors through centuries of history from the times when Natives camped here to the present day. You literally walk down the streets of 17th century Montreal. They have guided tours, an archeology field school, and the local businesses benefit as well.

According to the museums Web site:

*"On May 17, 1642, on a point of land at the confluence of the St. Lawrence and another, smaller river, Father Vimont held a mass celebrating the founding of Montréal, attended by Sieur de Maisonneuve, Jeanne Mance and their companions. On May 17, 1992, on the very same site, Pointe-à-Callière, the Montréal Museum of*

Underground Montreal draws over 400,000 thousand visitors annually.

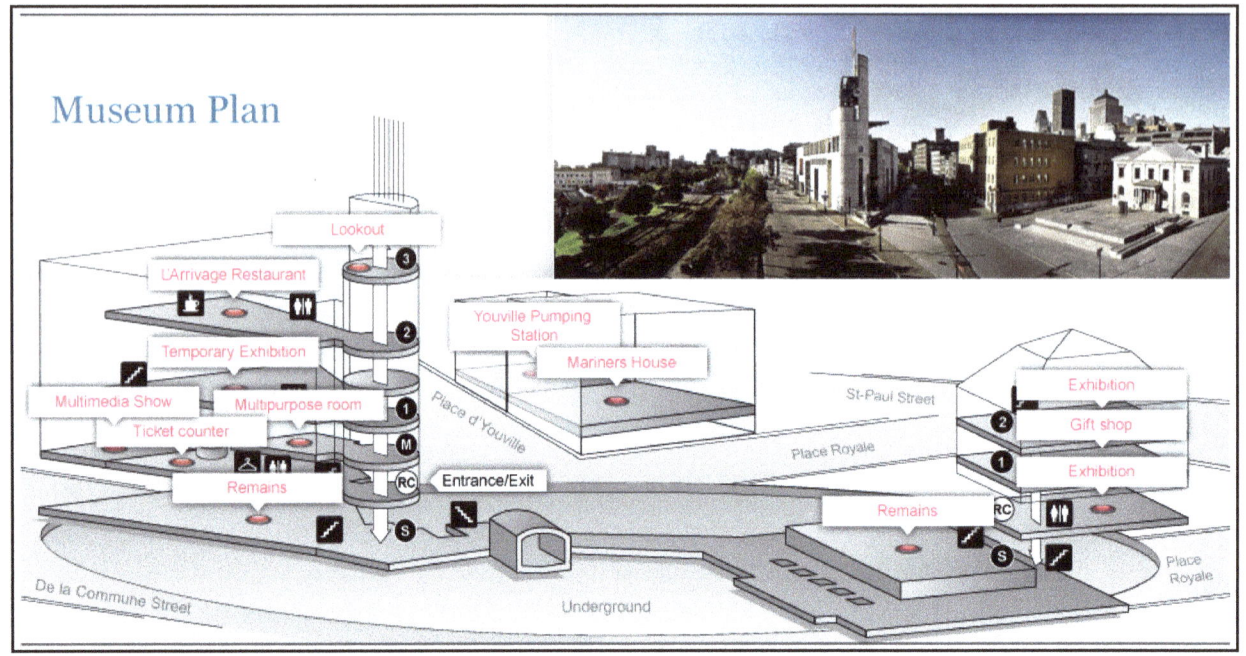

Museum plan in Montreal.

*Archaeology and History, opened its doors.*

*Until the Museum opened only historians knew about the "Pointe à Callière," so named because it was here that Chevalier Louis Hector de Callière, third governor of Montréal, had a home built in 1688. Today, the point has actually become part of the shoreline of the Island of Montréal, but its name lives on and is better known than ever, thanks to the Museum.*

*The Museum was founded as part of celebrations to mark Montréal's 350th birthday, and owes its existence largely to the significant archaeological discoveries made on the site during the 1980s. In fact, the Museum and its site are inextricably linked. Rising above evidence of more than 1,000 years of human activity, it houses remarkable architectural remains, displayed in situ with absolute respect for their integrity. Pointe-à-Callière is the only*

Thousamds of children each year learn about the founding of Montreal.

*sizable archaeology museum in Canada. The hundreds of artifacts it houses are grouped into six main sections: the Éperon, a modern building that has won many architectural awards; the archaeological crypt on the lower level; the renovated Ancienne-Douane building (Montréal's first Custom House), the Youville Pumping Station, the Archaeological Field School and the Mariners' House. The museum of a site, a history and a city, Pointe-à-Callière delves into the past to foster a debate on urban issues both local and global, and to encourage visitors to reflect on the future."*

Ironic, 2014 is the 400th anniversary of the founding of Albany with the building of Fort Nassau, on Castle Island, now Port of Albany.

Instead of duplicating Montreal's success, Fort Nassau may end up having an crude oil boiling facility on top of it.

Global Companies, a unit of Global Partners, based in Waltham, Massachusetts, plans to build a 2,600-square-foot facility at the port's rail yard to heat crude as it is pumped out of rail cars and into storage tanks. The oil will then be shipped out on barges headed downriver toward refineries on the East coast. Global's application does not specify what kind oil would be heated, but many worry it will be volatile tar sands from Canada.

The proposed boiler plant will have to be reviewed by the Albany Planning Board. The next planning board meeting is scheduled for Feb. 20, but so far the proposed boiler plant does not yet appear on the agenda. That means there's still time for the City of Albany to advocate for the best possible outcome. Comments on Global's project can be made to DEC through Karen M. Gaidasz, 1130 N. Westcott Road, Schenectady, NY 12306, or r4dep@gw.dec.state.ny.us. DEC is taking comments up to April 2 and there will be a DEC public hearing at Giffen Elementary on February 12, Wednesday at 6 PM.

And before the naysayers say something like this cannot happen in the United States, let me point them to Underground Seattle.

The **Seattle Underground** is a network of underground passageways and basements in downtown Seattle, Washington that was ground level at the city's origin in the mid-19th century. After the streets were elevated these spaces fell into disuse, but have become a tourist attraction in recent decades.

I also point you to the following articles in this book:

Underground Seattle draws over 400,000 thousand visitors annually. Photo from the Net.

The Albany Plan (of Preservation)

Welcome to the Albany Historium!

Such Promise But No Vision

# Such Promise But No Vision
First Published February 2, 2010, 11:36 am

The newest efforts to destroy more of Albany's history by the Fort Orange Club had me thinking about how other communities have embraced their history instead of destroying it. At first I thought it may be just smaller communities that cared because they have less historic resources but my research shows that size does not matter in this situation. Village, towns, cities, and even countries all have seen the value to save their history and even make money as a result. To this day Heritage Tourism is still the number one money maker in many countries.

According to the latest figures I could obtain from the US Travel Association:

In 2006, travel and tourism contributed $740 billion directly to the US economy. Travel and tourism is one of America's largest employers, employing more than 8 million people and creating a payroll income of $178 billion.

Visitors to historic sites and cultural attractions stay longer and spend more money than other kinds of tourists. Cultural and heritage visitors spend, on average, $623 per trip compared to $457 for all US travelers excluding the cost of transportation according to the Travel Industry of America. So the facts are there. What have other communities done? Let's take a look.

Preserving your history means saving archaeological resources also, which is the below ground history or prehistory of your area and not just standing structures. There are many good examples.

New York City for example when constructing the Stadt Huys Block in the 1970s-80s not only preserved Governor Lovelace's tavern foundation but constructed a glass topped opening complete with a brass railing around it so visitors could look and see it in place. It is a very popular tourist spot and is located across from the famous Frances Tavern.

When built the development covered two blocks obliterating the original Stone Street, the first street to be paved in the New Amsterdam. The developers incorporated the ground-floor hallway to follow the original street and a marker in the sidewalk at the entrance shows the old street plan. Paving marks the original curb and the foundations of two buildings that stood on the Pearl Street side of the block in colonial times. Pearl Street, named for an abundance of oysters, was once the original

Tourists viewing the Lovelace Tavern site. Photo by Don Rittner.

shoreline of Manhattan. Cream colored sidewalk stones on the block show the limits of New York's first city hall (Stadt huys).

When Old Montreal was discovered instead of putting a parking lot on top of it — like Albany likes to do - Montreal instead built a museum - *Pointe-à-Callière, the Montréal Museum of Archaeology and History* - on top of the site but incorporated the archaeologically uncovered city streets and buildings as part of the museum. Today you walk into a beautiful museum and then walk "down" into the original 17th century Montreal. When I visited the site in 2004, the museum had seen 317,000 visitors. More on this concept later.

It doesn't stop there in Montreal. In the 1980s, Christ Church, a Cathedral that was completed in 1859 and based on the design of British architect Frank Wills was in serious state of disrepair. In order to save the church they decided to build underneath the church a retail mall. It became the Cathedral on Stilts as they dug new foundations and created a multi-million dollar office adjacent and retail space below it. There is also a 10,000 sq. ft. Mezzanine floor sandwiched between the Cathedral floor and the ceiling of the first retail level. The retail development under the Cathedral, its grounds, and two of

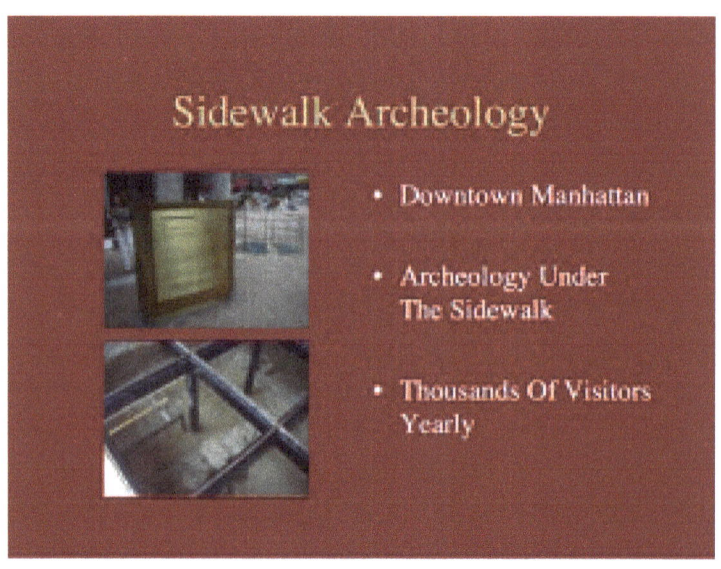

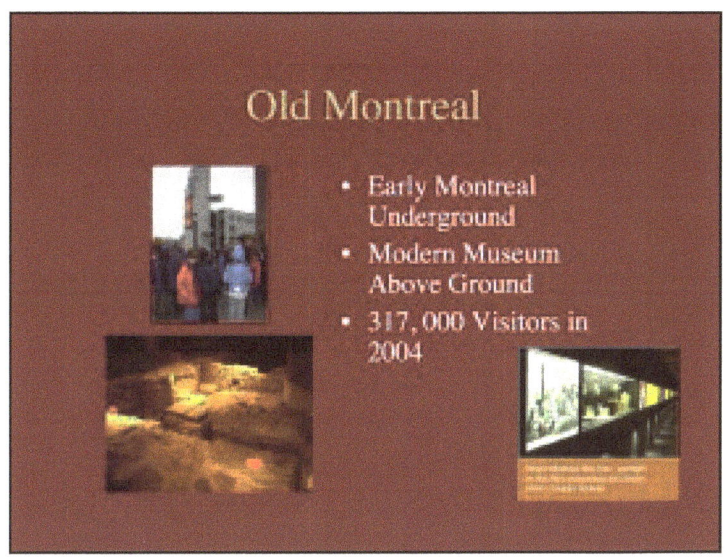

the surrounding streets were opened in the fall of 1988.

Also in Montreal is the first stone church known as the *Chapel Notre-Dame-de-Bonsecours* and was built in 1675. The Chapel was destroyed by fire in 1754. In 1766, the new British authorities made a request to buy the chapel lands to build more spacious barracks for the garrison. The Sulpician's and the fabrique of Notre-Dame intervened to save the site and announced their intention of building a new chapel over the original foundations. The chapel built in 1771 is the one that exists today. However when they were excavating the found the remains of the palisade of 1709 beneath the chapel and other remains of the original chapel. What did they do? You guess it. They saved it and you can visit the original remains which includes the burial of some of the sisters of the original chapel.

Back in the US, Seattle, Washington had a fire in 1889 ending in the destruction of 25 city blocks, much of the downtown area. Many of the streets ended up being as high as 32 feet above the ground floors of the surrounding buildings and people literally had to use ladders to climb up or down to get across the street. To remedy these new problems, various bridges and sidewalks were eventually built, effectively burying the ground floors.

Today you can roam the subterranean passages that once were the main roadways and first-floor storefronts of old downtown Seattle. In May 1970, the Seattle City Council adopted an ordinance naming 20 square blocks in Pioneer Square a Historic District. Later, Pioneer Square became the city's first neighborhood to be so listed in the National Register of Historic

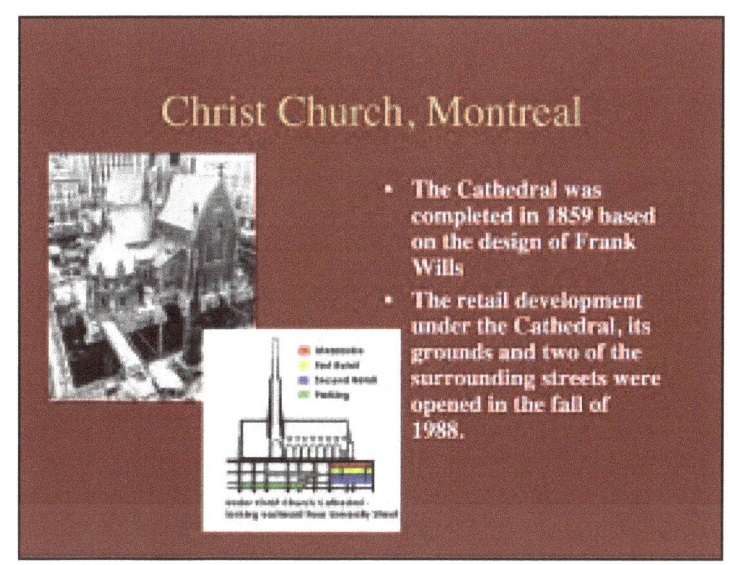

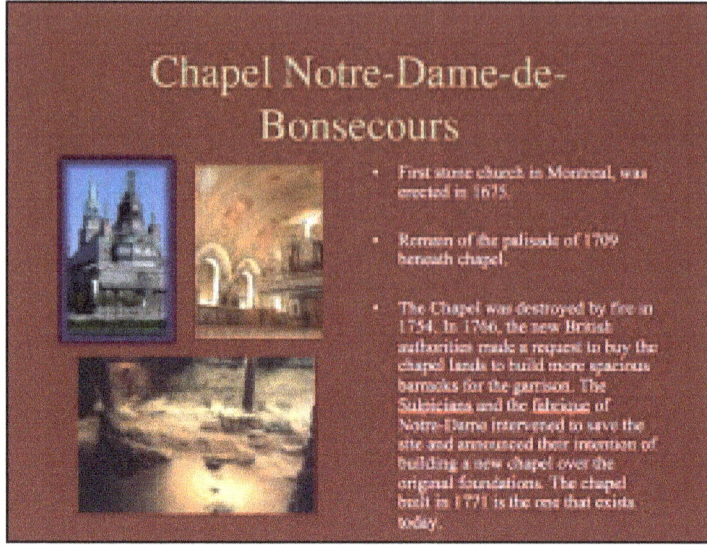

Places. In 1965, local citizen Bill Speidel established "Bill Speidel's Underground Tour" and took customers on a tour of what was left underneath Pioneer Square, paying rent to the building owners for the privilege. The tour is still very popular.

In Mexico, digging by workers from the electric company in 1978 found the remains of that country's history. The El Temple Mayor is a major Aztec Temple in Technotitlan (now Ciudad de Mexico). It has 7 pyramids, one inside another. The Circular pyramid is dedicated to the Aztec God of wind, Ehécatl. Instead of moving it out and placing it in a museum, it was left in the place it was found. So, around this pyramid, the *Pino Suárez* station (lines 1 and 2) was built. As a tribute, the pyramid was chosen as the station's symbol. The pyramid can be seen on display along the main transfer corridor.

The remains of a mammoth (dated 10,000 BC), while digging the soil for building the Talismán station are shown permanently in site.

In fact subway tunnel and station excavations often turn up archaeological resources, and to this day twenty-seven subway stations in a dozen countries have those resources available for viewing.

In Athens, when the city expanded its metro to accommodate the 2004 Olympics, 30,000 artifacts were found scattered beneath 17 acres.

During construction, a 11th or 13th-century shipwreck was discovered at Yenikapi, what had been a harbor in Byzantine Istanbul.

Mexican temple in the train station. Photo from Wikipedia.

Approximately 2,000 fossils (mastodon, camel, ground sloth) dating back 16.5 million years were located way beneath the surface of Los Angeles.

Construction of Line 14 of the Paris metro unearthed canoe-shaped boats 32 feet below the banks of the Seine, dating to about 2,800-2,500 BC, hinting at what may be the earliest human settlement in the area. (According to an article in National Geographic by Meg Weaver http://blogs.nationalgeographic.com/blogs/intelligenttravel/2009/11/what-the-metro-unearthed.html).

That brings us back to Albany. In 2001, almost a decade ago, historian John Wolcott and I drafted a plan for saving underground Albany. We called it the Beverwyck Archeological Park. This included a plan to uncover many of the important archeological features we know exist (and where). The plan was submitted to the city which quickly rushed to do nothing.

The city has historically ignored its archeological treasures. So many opportunities have been lost starting with the very start of the city - Fort Orange - itself being covered over by the off ramp of I-787 in the early 70s. During the early part of this new century, Albany's old stockades, house sites, ports,

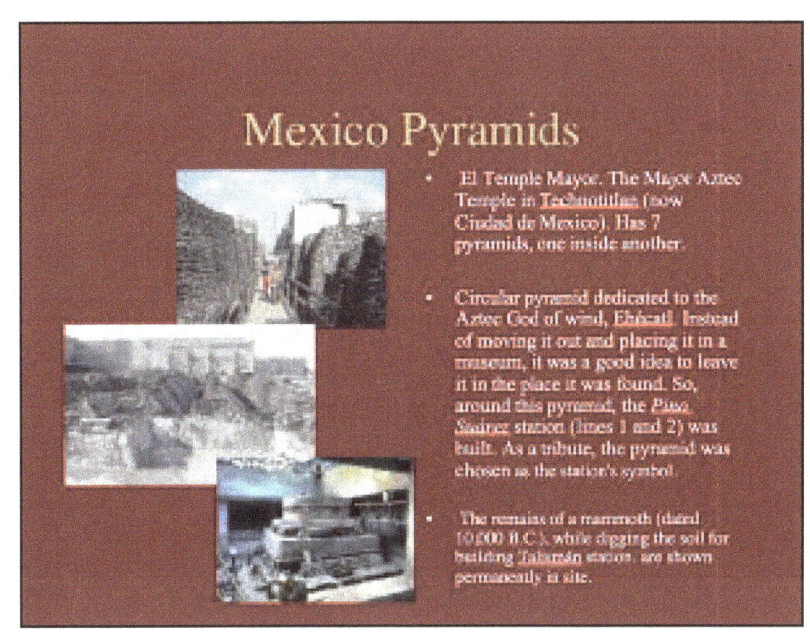

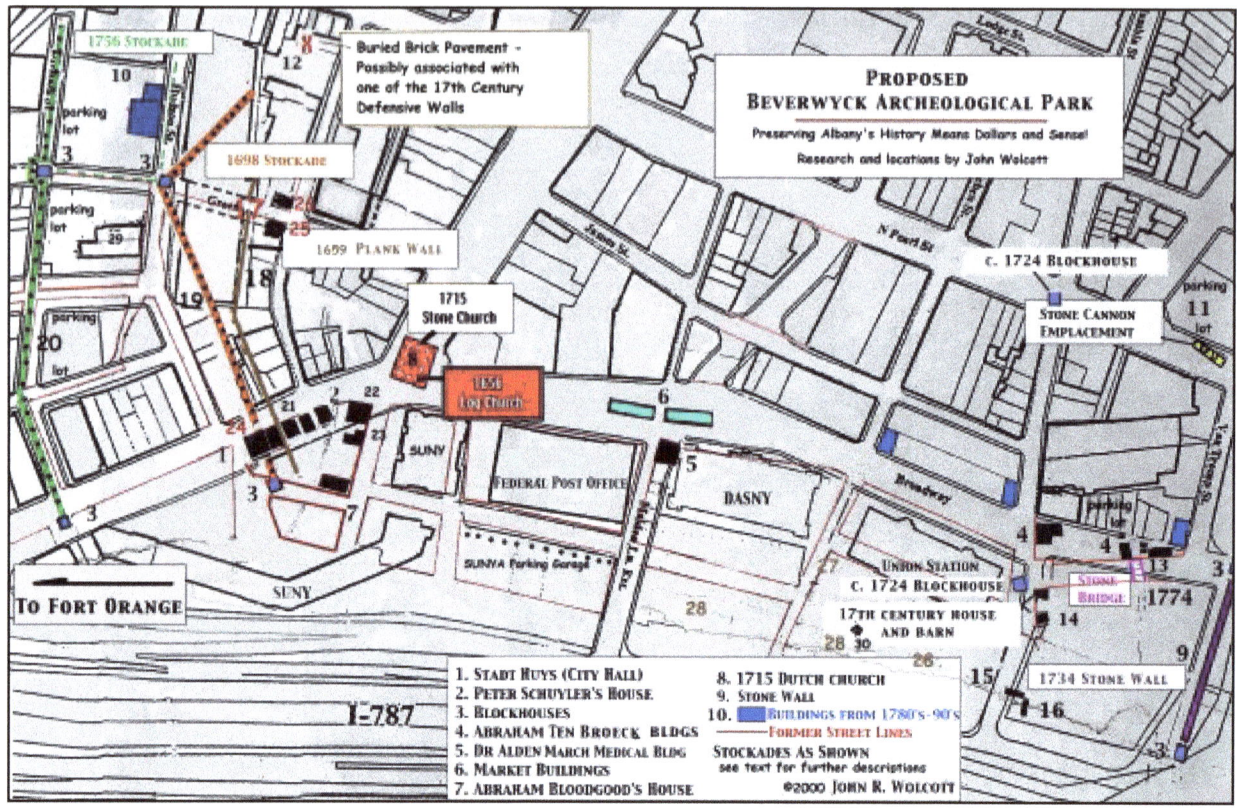

Proposed archeological park by Rittner and Wolcott.

businesses, distilleries and Native American artifacts have been found and quickly covered over by parking lots, roads, and buildings. They can never be recovered and so much of what millions of people would have paid to see are gone forever. A city with no appreciation of its past is a city that has a perilous future.

# Another Removal of Albany History Hits the Road
First published on December 6, 2013 2:07 pm

My first history/archeology project back in 1972 was relocating and preserving the Kings's Highway, the first road between the Hudson and Mohawk Valleys that connected Albany (Fort Orange) to Schenectady (Skenectada). I took up the unfinished work of Schenectady City Historian William Efner who began this project back in the 1930s. Fortunately I was able to save a mile long section of the original sandy road when Mayor Corning purchased the first city Pine Bush Preserve back in the late 70s at my request.

In 1975, I was able to erect more than 20 historic markers along this route and all but one still exist along the original route beginning at City Hall in Albany and ending on Ferry Street in Schenectady (should be at Church Street and I have been trying to get

The original King's Highway, oldest road in Albany was preserved thanks to Mayor Corning when I asked him to buy this parcel for preservation in 1975. Google Map.

Road Street. Photo by Don Rittner

the city to move it for years). So I have an interest in early colonial roads and their importance in the growth and development of the Hudson and Mohawk Valleys.

Albany historian John Wolcott has been trying to call attention to what may be the second oldest road in Albany, at least second in that there is — or I should say was — an original part of it in downtown Albany. I just witnessed its partial destruction by Habitat for Humanity. They have ripped out half of it for a development along Sheridan Avenue and Dove Street for what the Dutch may have called the "Vossen Kill Clove" since it is the valley of the Vossen Kill or Fox Creek named for Andries de Vos. Vos is Dutch for fox, so it is named for a person and not directly for the animal that is still erroneously attributed to by historians as discovered by historian Wolcott. The original Dutch document called it the old foxes kill, meaning the old fox, a nickname for Andries de Vos and is really not pertaining to the stream but rather to the person it's named for.

It has not fallen by the wayside either to Albany native and writer Paula Lemire who wrote about the road a few years ago in her Albany History Blog (http://albanynyhistory.blogspot.com/2010/08/relic-of-road.html)

It is called "Road Street" although its original name was likely the Vossen Kill Road, but in 1762 the Common Council called it "the road to the Schyt Berghie" and is the only early unpaved colonial street in downtown Albany and along with the original portion of the King's Highway the only original remnants of our colonial overland transportation routes in original condition. The Vossen Kill Road began, well at the end of the kill, close to the Hudson, and moved up past North Pearl Street just north of Columbia as an alley then worked its way up Sheridan Hollow and formed the lower portion of present Sheridan Avenue or Road Street. The road went through a gate in the city stockade where Sheridan and North Pearl now meet and then moved up the hollow and found its way to Dung Hill (Schuyt Berghie) located where Townsend Park is now situated. Dung hill is where they deposited, well, you know, dung. They certainly didn't want it smelling up the neighborhoods downtown. What is also interesting is Dung Hill was actually one of the ancient parabolic sand dunes that formed the Pine Bush, now located several miles west. Yes, the Pine Bush actually began down near Pine Street close to City Hall. Dung Hill may be the eastern most sand dune located on a map. It is also pointed in the right direction having its axis facing in the direction of the prevailing wind that formed it (from the West). The next known dune is at the three mile house (tavern) that was located where Swinburne Park is today. The rise you see in the park is actually a Pine Bush sand dune and was

Romer Map of 1698 shows the Fox Kill (#6 on map) laid out in farm lots with buildings. Number 20 is the tanning houses.

called the "Eerste Santbergh."

Road Street was an important road because many industries sprang up in Sheridan Hollow: brick making, tanners, and perhaps potters utilizing the clay from the stream bed (and post glacial events like Lake Albany deposits). Important enough that in 1762 the residents petitioned the common council to leave the road open! The council also wrote on April 27 *"...ordered that none of the Shoemakers that have their tan pitts in Foxes Creek, throw none of their old tan in or near said creek..."* While this apparent environmental concern seems early, it should be pointed out that Ben Franklin was complaining about their smell and pollution some 20 years before this in Philadelphia. Franklin wrote: *"As the Tanners who own Land on the Dock are very few, and the People whose Interest is affected by their Remaining there, are a very great Number, the Damage done to others, and to the City, by their Continuing where they are."* Some would say a very socialist view, but repeated in 1914 by Albany architect Arnold Brunner about the Pine Bush – but that is subject for another story for another day. Back to Road Street

So it appears that Habitat for Humanity was allowed to destroy this portion of the historic roadbed and ironically Wolcott and I are probably the last people to ride over the road as we took a ride down the road about a week ago and I filmed it which you

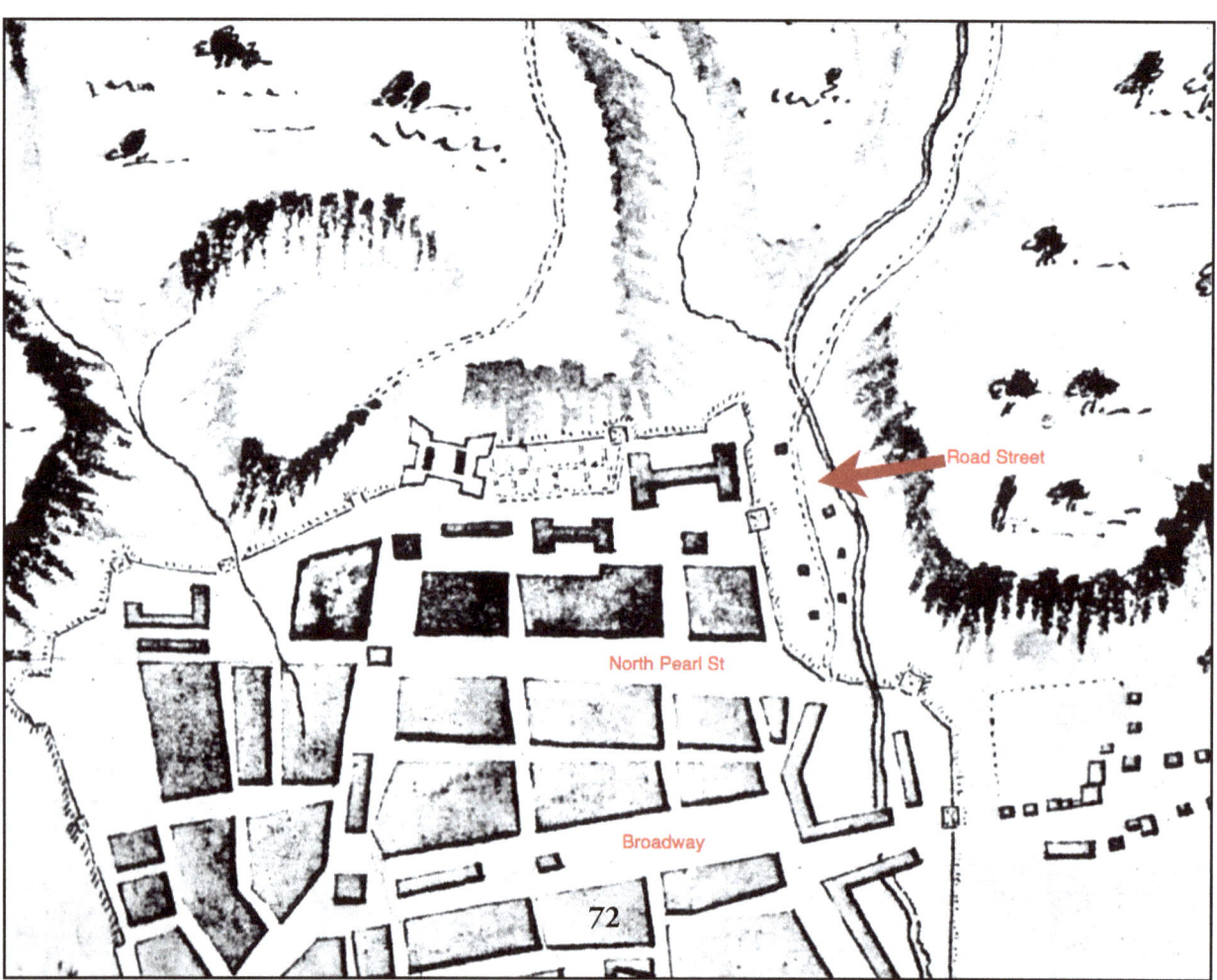

1758 Map of Albany showing Road Street and buildings.

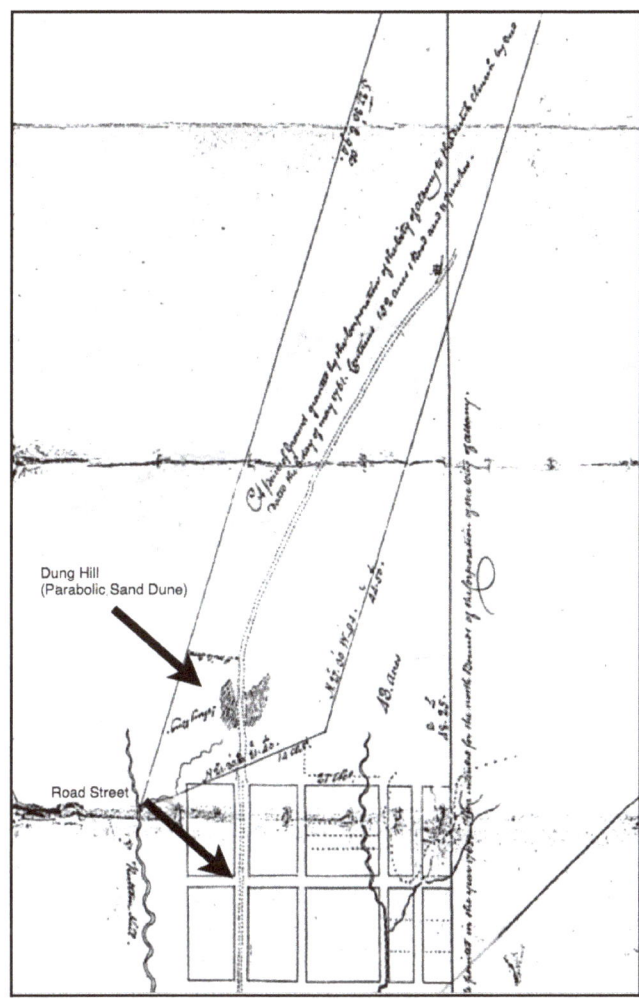

A 1775 map showing Road Street going to Dung Hill (now Townsend Park area). Actually a Pine Bush sand dune. This may be the earliest map showing a sand dune. Courtesy John Wolcott.

can see here (make take a few moments to load — big file).
http://www.donrittner.com/RoadStreet.MOV

I know that not enough people are going to care about this historic road bed being destroyed. However, I am simply amazed how a city that is closing in at four hundred years old continues to neglect its history — one that very few American cities can brag about, let alone continually destroy.

In conclusion. I wonder is this site being developed for housing considered a brown field from airborne deposition from the nearby former Answers Plant? Was it remediated?

Why was there no archeological survey conducted on the site, since there were known early 17th century industries and buildings and history being made in the hollow, and in particular a row of buildings right on this site? We know that didn't happen or the road would still be there. Or if it did I would like to read the report and how they justified this act, and how a city archeologist review would not have caught this? Ironically, at the request for public input in a public forum (Charette) by Habitat for Humanity John Wolcott presented his extensive (A Brief Review of Their Contexual Background in the Valley of the Vossen Kill) research on Sheridan Hollow that he did for Interfaith Alliance through Landmark Archeology. They did an archeological survey for 175-77 Sheridan Avenue which is practically across the street from this development site (175 was rehabbed). It contains a great deal of historical documentation on the settlement and industrial use of the Hollow during the 17th and 18th centuries and right up through the 20th century. So no one can say that they didn't know there was important historical and scenic resources on this site.

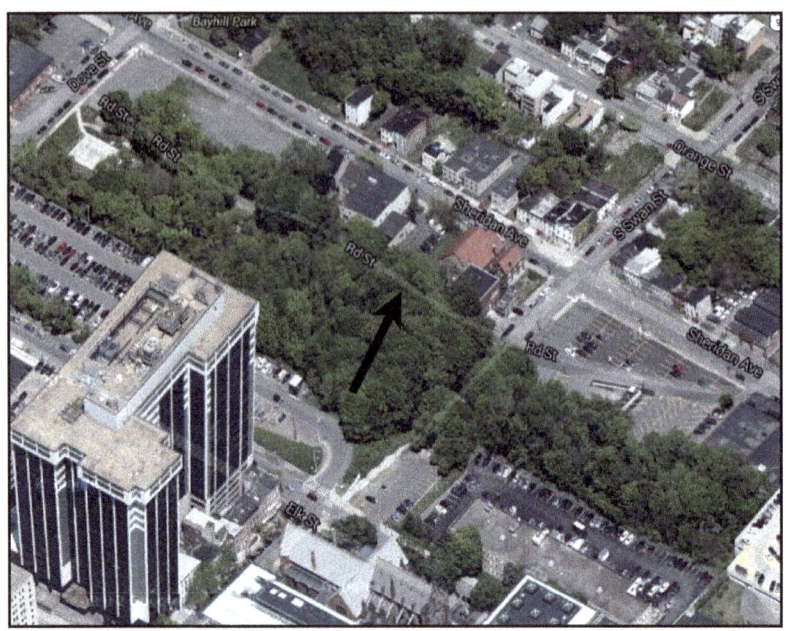

Aerial of Road Street. What is amazing is that the service road into the parking lot where it begins follows the original route. Google Map.

The city has had a city archeologist position in the law since I believe 2003 (I was the first in the country in 1973 and for Albany but they seemed to have lost that ordinance over the past 40 years) and they had an Old World archeologist from SUNYA as their archeologist for a short time. I'm not knocking him. Just saying there is a difference between Old World and Northeastern prehistory. The city has not had a practicing archeologist as far as I can tell for years even though there was a significant budget appropriated each year for it. And sadly, this upcoming budget has completely removed the position, which I believe goes against their own laws which require archeological review by a city archeologist?

And why was the historic road allowed to be destroyed in the first place. Why could that not have been incorporated into the plan and used as is for a secondary route, or better yet, a walking trail in honor of its history?

Sadly, only half of the road now exists — and who knows for how long.

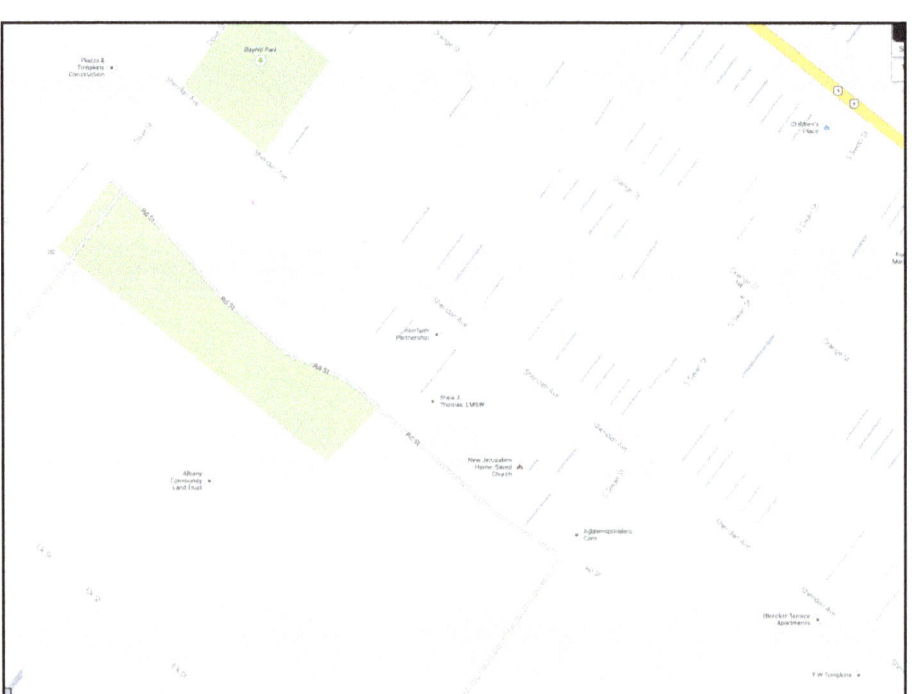

Here is a plan view of Road Street from Google Maps.

Jacob Lansing House, corner of Columbia and North Pearl, built in 1710, had as its back boundary the road to the Vos Kill. This house is where Natives stayed when trading. Torn down in the 1890s.

See that alley way with car parked in it? It is the original Road Street as it came up from the river and crossed North Pearl Street and then going into the hollow. Google Map.

Albany has a law that specifically states that the city archeologist will , *"review all development plans which involve potential archeological sites, conduct preliminary assessments of the potential archeological significance of any site plan area and of the impact of any proposed ground-disturbing activities on such area, and make recommendations as to the necessity of cultural resource investigations."*

I also believe that the city's Historic Resource Commission must have an archeologist on it. I believe they do not have one.

There have been several goof ups in the last few weeks because they city has failed to consider archeological impact with no archeologist onboard: the 18th century Paul Clark Tavern (Tandor Palace) on Madison and Lark; A development KIPP Tech Valley Charter School off Dudley Heights (The report was done by a Pennsylvania firm and inadequate in my opinion) on the old Dudley Observatory hill; and now this Habitat for Humanity Project which has adversely impacted 17th century remains. There are probably more.

Corner of Dove and Sheridan where Habitat housing is going. You can see Road Street delineated. The top half is now gone. Google Maps.

So there you have it. Albany has laws in place for archeological review and they don't do it in defiance (or perhaps ignorance) of their own laws, and now have even defunded the position that could do it.

In the meantime, more and more of the city's irreplaceable treasures get tossed.

# Welcome to the Albany Historium!
First published on July 7, 2013

Seems like the convention center is dead in the water and there are folks offering suggestions for redevelopment of the land that was formerly Beverwyck, the first incorporated village that originally surrounded Fort Orange in 1652, now Albany. Too bad they tore down all those great historic buildings before they decided it was a bad idea.

Here is a better plan. Why not create something that will allow people to live, shop, and visit this site, and encourage tourists to come and spend their money? We can stick with the maritime theme. Create the Albany Historium! In a nutshell it is:

- A seaport on the Hudson River that can accommodate several historic ships. About 700 feet away from the former convention site.

- Entrance way into the Historium flanked by retail and apartments.

- A reconstructed full size replica of Fort Orange to draw tourists and guide visitors to all the great historic sites in the city and surrounding region

- The excavation and exhibit of the remaining section of the real Fort Orange under Broadway that will really draw tourists.

- The Albany Aquarium

- Condos and apartments.

- New Beverwyck Village, a retail, commercial and residential three block area designed in 17th Century Dutch style along with an underground exploratorium.

- Historic Albany Foundation Van Ostrand Dutch House Orientation Center.

- Liberty Park and Archeology Center.

- Mohican Casino and IMAX Theater with a museum about the early Mohican history before Europeans arrived.

- Bus Station, or if needed extension of casino.

- Bus Station. Use the old Greyhound instead of Trailways if option 11 is used.

- A wooden stockade wall to mimic the original stockade that surrounded the village. Also acts as a buffer or screen off the elevated highway system.

- Beverwyck Archeological Park (See my earlier column)

- Parking

- More Hotel

- Ticket Office for Historic Dock Street.

## 1. Historic Dock Street Seaport

Boy we are really missing the boat on this one — literally. This is a no brainer. Right now the World War II Destroyer Escort the USS Slater is docked along the river just north of the old Albany Hardware Store (now U-Haul storage, formerly Albany Hardware, but would make great condos). It is the last destroyer escort afloat and is open for tours from April to November. It has over 2500 members around the

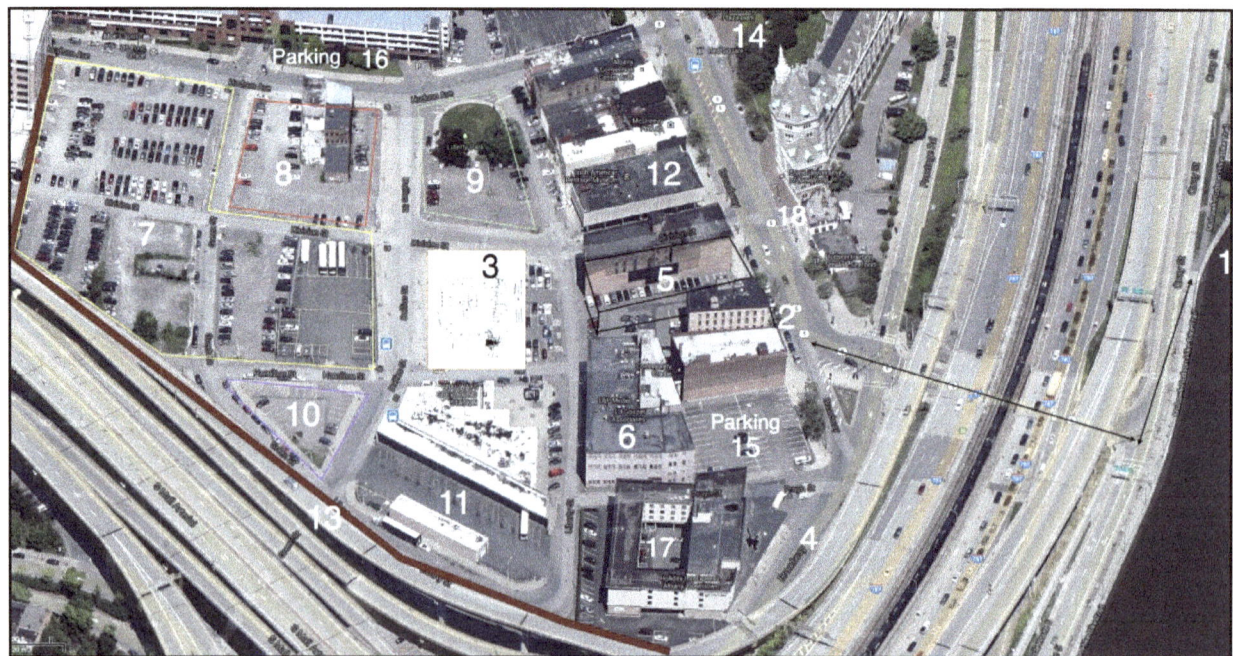

The Historium Plan by Don Rittner. See numbered descriptions.

The Onrust replica. First Dutch fur trading ship built in America. The original visited Albany area in 1614 and members of Captain Adriaen Block's crew built Fort Nassau on Castle Island (now Port of Albany) which is the beginning of Albany's European history.

country and thousands visit each year. There are presently several historic ships that could also dock here for extended periods of time and attract thousands of visitors. There is the Onrust, the replica of the first fur trading ship built in America in 1614, now at the Waterford Visitors Center. Built by more than 250 local volunteers, it was the voyages of this ship that explored the entire coast between Cape Cod and Delaware Bay and was responsible for the Dutch settling in what was known as New Netherland - including Albany. It was part of the crew from the Onrust's captain Adriaen Block that founded Fort Nassau, the beginning of Albany on Castle Island (now Port of Albany). It is known that the Onrust visited Fort Nassau while it was being built in 1614. There is the Half Moon, a replica of Henry Hudson's ship that explored in 1609 looking for the Northwest Passage. The Sloop Clearwater was launched in 1969 under the guidance of legendary folk hero Pete Seeger to call

The Half Moon Replica.

attention to the environmental degradation of the Hudson. There is the smaller sloop the Woody Guntrie launched in 1978 that provides rides and education. The Schooner Mystic Whaler is a replica of the late 19th century coastal cargo boats built in 1967 and rebuilt in 1993. The Lois McClure is a replica of an 1862 Schooner. All of the ships provide education, some provide rides, and all provide a history lesson from the beginning of our European presence in the Albany area to World War II. I have no doubt that all of these ships would spend some time along a new dock that would have slips just for them. Imagine seeing these ships going up and down the Hudson and providing exciting educational experiences for young and old. The dock should be placed near the Albany Riverfront Park and run south. The former Albany Aquaducks center office could be used for ticket sales for the historic boats, or how about using the original ticket office building on Broadway that was used for the old Day Liners. After visiting the seaport visitors could then walk about 1000 feet to the entrance to the Historium on Broadway.

## 2. Historium Grand Entrance

Number 2 and 4 E-Comm place are two 19th century buildings that could easily be converted to condos or apartments with retail on the first floor. A connecting sign between the two would welcome visitors and lead them to the reconstructed Fort Orange and the end of the street (old Hamilton Street).

Entrance to Historium area from Historic Dock Street Seaport.

Entrance way to Historium. Large sign connecting both buildings would be placed here. Buildings could be apartments or retail or combo.

## 3. Fort Orange Replica

Historic Dock Street Seaport. Imagine docks with five or more historic ships here along the river.

Entrance to Dock Street Seaport from Historium on Broadway.

The parcel situated between Liberty, Division, Dallius, and Hamilton can be used to build a replica of Fort Orange. This would be a major attraction and teach visitors about the early Dutch history of the city. It could also serve as a go to point to be directed to all the historic sites in the city such as Cherry Hill, Schuyler Mansion, Shaker site, Ten Broeck Mansion, Fort Crailo, etc.

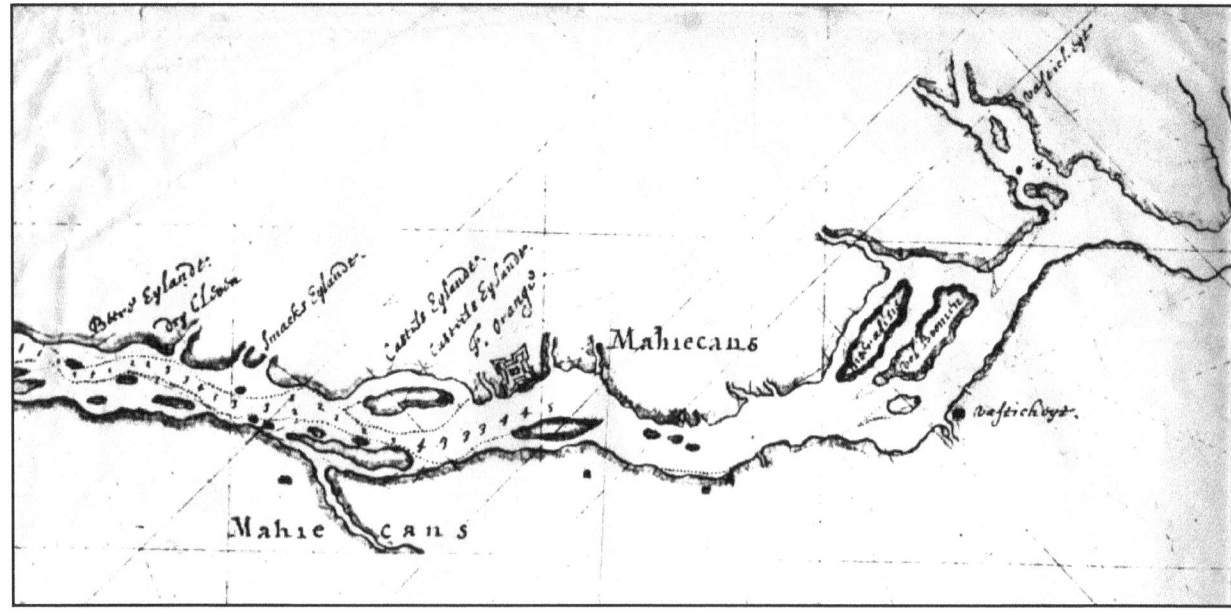
Fort Orange location on 1631 map.

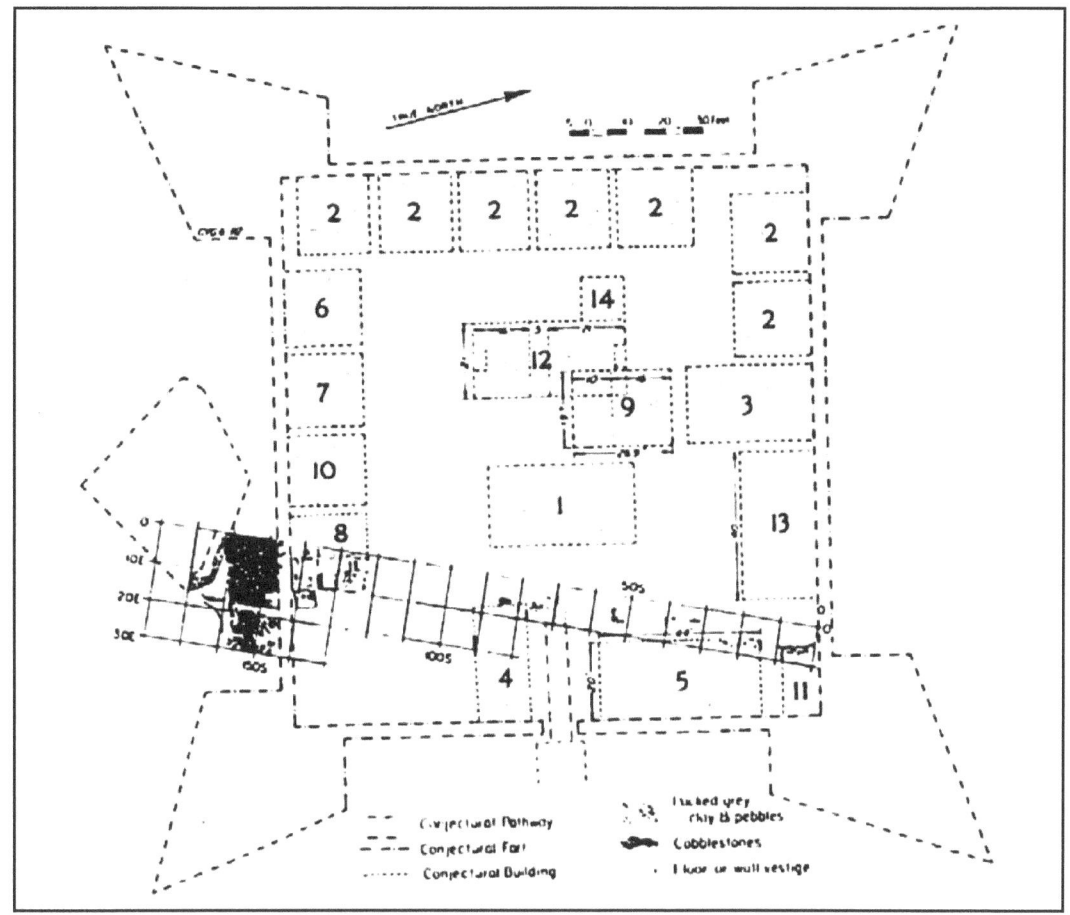

Fort Orange. A replica Fort would be built behind the entrance way in the area of Liberty and Dallius Streets.

## 4. The Real Fort Orange

In the early 1970s part of the original Fort Orange was excavated and then the off-ramp for the highway was placed on top of it. There is still a sizable part of the original fort including a bastion that lies under Broadway. Broadway could be closed off here, the site excavated, and used in the interpretation at the Fort Orange replica.

## 5. The Albany Aquarium

Ok, there is some interest in this and I have no objections since we are building on a marine theme in the first place. A good

1970 excavations of Fort Orange now covered by road ramp.

The original Fort Orange is waiting to be excavated under Broadway. The ramp on the left is on top of it and was partially excavated when the ramp was being built.

place for an aquarium is between 4 and 6 E-Comm Buildings. The Aquarium could be tied into one of the buildings and act as the educational component similar to the other aquariums around the country that have special dioramas or areas that teach about a specific water ecosystem. I would have part of the front on Broadway be glass so the passerby could see some of the fish.

### 6. Condos, Apartments and Retail Space

Several of the buildings standing can be converted to condos and apartments. Let's face it you need to have people living in the downtown again and this is a great place to do it.

Dallas World Aquarium as an example. From the Net.

84

A sizable population would then demand other services and increase the desire to redevelop and live in the inner city again.

## 7. New Beverwyck

The western most section of the area that encompasses Division, Hudson, Green, Hamilton and Dallius should be used to build a mix of 17th century looking Dutch buildings that will be a mix of residential, commercial and retail. However the catch is

Several aquariums around the country could be used as a model for Albany. From the Net.

that the area will be excavated archeologically and the village be built over the excavated area. This would be similar to Underground Seattle and The Museum of Archeology in Montreal (390,000+ visitors last year) where the early parts of the city were excavated and new structures built on top. Here visitors could explore the interconnected ruins of 17th century Beverwyck but also be able live, shop, and eat above.

Broadway would be transformed into a vibrant tourist attraction.

## 8. Historic Albany Foundation Van Ostrand House Interpretative Center

Ok, someone has to be able to coordinate all this history and since Historic Albany Foundation is now the owner of the earliest Dutch house in existence at 48 Hudson, they should be given 50 Hudson as well and they can use this not only as their offices but create an interpretive center where all this great history can be taught and coordinated with tours, etc. If Kathy Sheehan becomes the next Mayor, HAF may get to actually be able to work with an administration that gets the economic sense of historic preservation.

48 Hudson Avenue, Albany, NY

## 9. Liberty Park

Liberty Park should be expanded by excavating the area that is now parking and incorporate into the existing park. There could be some interesting outdoor cafes here.

## 10. The Mohican Casino and IMAX Theater

The area that bounds the South Mall Arterial and the triangular piece of Green, Hamilton, and Dallius Streets can be used to build a casino and IMAX Theater. The casino should be run by the Mohican Nation.

Yes folks they still exist, contrary to

New Beverwyck consists of 17th century styled structures that contain apartments and retail along present historic Albany streets. From the Net.

Seattle Underground tours see thousands of visitors each year. From the

James Fennimore Cooper, and considering it was the Mohicans who allowed the Dutch to build their fort here in the first place, consider it a bit of a payback. Since the Albany area was approved by the State legislature as a possible site, here is the location. The Mohican's have a successful casino in Wisconsin so they know how to

North Star Mohican Casino. The Mohican Nation should be given first chance to build a casino here. After all it was the Mohicans who gave the Dutch permission to build here in the first place.

do it. A museum in the casino will give the history of the Mohican Nation that lived here before Europeans arrived. North Star Mohican Casino. The Mohicans should be given first chance to build a casino here. After all it was the Mohicans who gave the Dutch permission to build here in the first place.

### 11 & 12. The Bus Station

Underground Montreal. The Museum Pointe-A-Calliere. Here you walk through a modern museum and walk down into the earlier excavated 17th century original city.

The existing Trailways Greyhound station can be upgraded to act as a perfect place for tourists around the country to come and visit the Historium. Or better yet, this space could be used for the casino and IMAX theater and the old Greyhound station (Number 12 on the map) be brought back to life.

### 13 The Stockade

Outdoor cafe's in New Beverwyck.

I find the vista looking south pretty ugly. A way to mitigate the unsightly South Mall Arterial would be to build a stockade running the length of it. The original Beverwyck was surrounded by one and this could be part of the interpretive history.

### 14. Beverwyck Archeological Park

The Historium can be a

Original Stockade posts from Albany. A replica stockade set up on the south side of the project area would help take the eye off the ugly South Mall arterial.

part of my earlier proposed Beverwyck archaeological park that would uncover the first city hall, where Ben Franklin outlined the Plan of Union, Peter Schuyler, Albany's first mayor house and a host of other great sites. See my piece on The Albany Plan of Preservation — Preserving Albany's Undiscovered City.

### 15 & 16. Parking

Yes you need parking but there already is a garage on Hudson that you could probably add a few floors to and the parking lot at Broadway and Pruyn could get a new multilevel garage.

### 17. Hotel Rooms

So where would visitors stay when visiting? The Holiday Inn Express is right on the corner. Perhaps the hotel could expand if more rooms were needed.

### 18. Albany Maritime Dock Ticket Office

The building just south of the D&H Building on Broadway was the original ticket office when steamboats plied the Hudson River. It is now vacant and could be reused as a ticket office for the historic ships.

If this proposal ever saw the light of day, it would transform Albany and make it a destination city instead of a stop over. I won't hold my breath.

An IMAX theater attached or part of a casino would bring state of

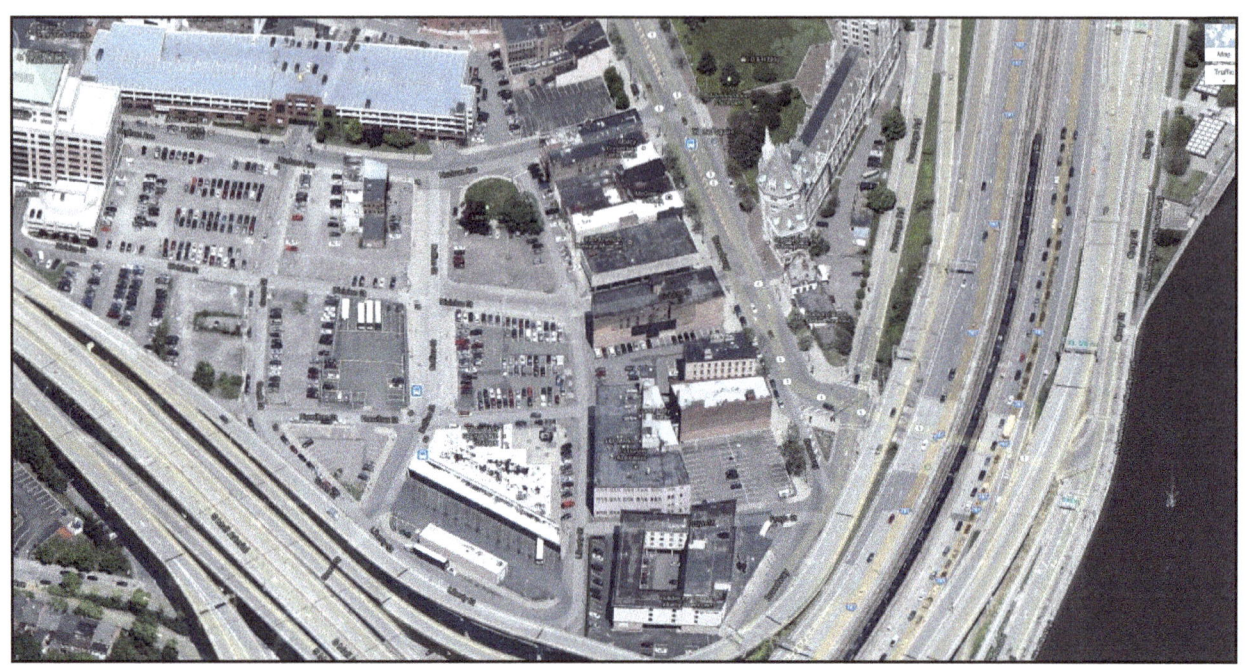
Aerial of proposed Albany Historium.

Riverside Park was created in 1901 along the Hudson below Westerlo Street. It disappeared before World War II.

# Boiling plant threatens the Most Important Historic Archeological Site in the Northeast United States

First Published on January 26, 2014 2:18 am

The Port of Albany is not what it seems. While today it is the location of scrap yards, molasses storage, grain elevators, and other industrial sites, the Port's opening in 1932 was not the first commercial use of the land.

Before the opening of the Port it was an island and over the years had several names from Castle Island, Martine Gerritse's land, Patroon's Island, Van Rensselaer Island, to more recently Westerlo Island.

This island became the focus for the first Dutch habitation in the New World when a group of sailors built a fort and defensive structure on the northern part of the island in 1614, and named it Fort Nassau. This was the beginning of Albany. It was also proof that the Dutch and Mohican Nation that controlled the area had good relations.

The founding of Fort Nassau was a result of the 1613 trading expedition under the overall command of Captain Adriaen Block working for the Amsterdam Van Tweenhysen Company. Block commanded the ship the *Tiger* while Hedrick Christiaensen commanded the *Fortune*. Both ships, along with a third named the *Nightingale*, belonging to a second company, were moored somewhere in New York Bay during the winter of 1613.

Block's ship the *Tiger* burned in December 1613 or early January 1614, and they set out to build a new ship, *The Onrust*, with his remaining crew. Block sent Christiaensen and his crew up the Hudson River to build a trading post, Fort Nassau.

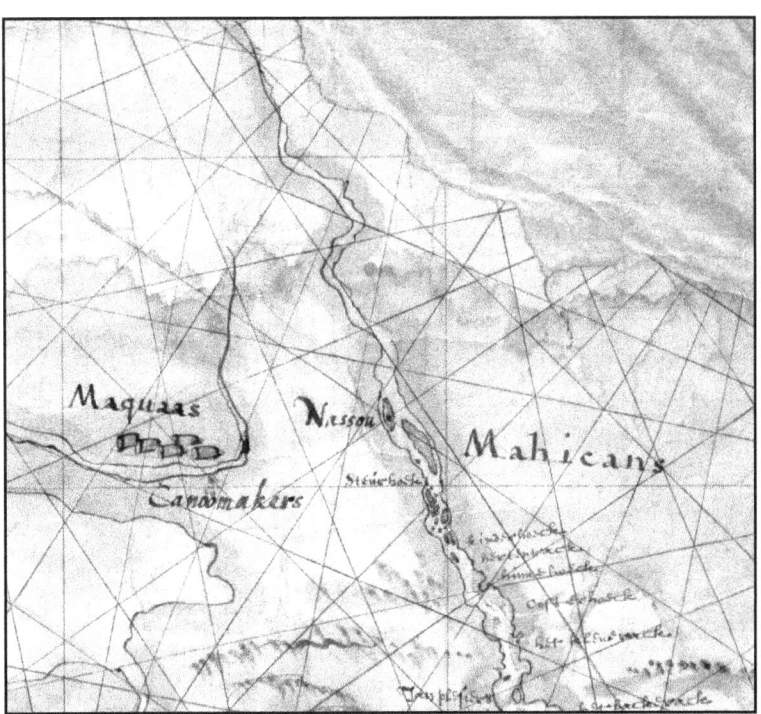

Cornelis Hendrickson's 1616 map showing location of Fort Nassau. This is Albany today.

Christiaensen and his men selected the North part of Castle Island and built the Fort that was 58 feet by 58 feet (interior dimensions), and surrounded it with a moat eighteen feet wide. The moat along with breastworks protected a trading house 38 feet by 28 feet. It became the focal point for the North American fur trade in the Northeast. It also became the staging point for expeditions to seek out mineral deposits and other natural resources for exploitation.

After several washouts by the Hudson River spring floods, and a final severe one in 1617, the Dutch moved on to the mainland and built Fort Orange, which in 1970 was partially excavated before an exit from I-787 was placed on top of it.

While Fort Nassau was abandoned, the island became the home for several farms; the first called Rensselaerburgh was leased in 1630. Other tenants on the island were Brant Peelen, Adriaen Vanderdonck, first Sheriff in the Dutch colony and first promoter of democracy in the new world, Cornelis Segerse, and Martin Gerrittse Van Bergen. The farm sites may also be available on the island for archeological exploration.

By the 18th century, the island was called Patroon's Island and was leased to John Bradstreet. Upon the death of the Patroon, the land became the property of his wife Catherine who may have renamed it Westerlo after her new husband Dominie Eilardus Westerlo in 1775. By the 19th century it not only was producing crops but two ironworks occupied the northern part.

In 1909 Albany became the first city to have a public airport when part of the island became an airfield called Quenton Roosevelt Field (after the president's son who was killed in WW I) and famous aviators

1639 map showing location of abandoned Fort Nassau and Fort Orange on the mainland.

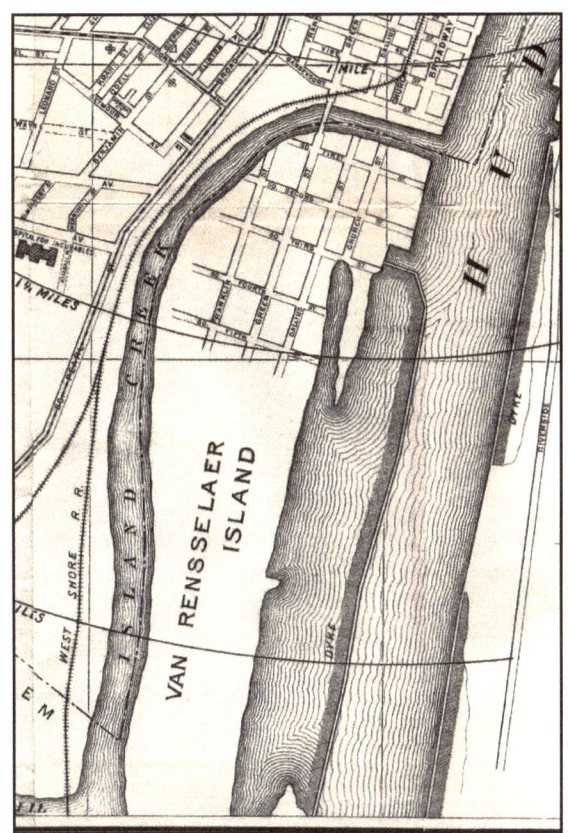

Van Rensselaer Island 1908. Now Port of Albany.

such as Amelia Earhart, James Doolittle, Clarence Chamberlain, Glenn Curtiss and Charles Lindbergh landed here. Lindbergh landed his "Spirit of St. Louis" at 2:06 PM on July 27, 1927, shortly after his historic flight to Paris, and was greeted on the island by 10,000 people.

Curtiss on May 29, 1910, left Albany and flew to Manhattan down the Hudson making the first true cross country flight in the United States.

In 1931 the Albany Port Authority was created and filling and dredging began until the Port of Albany, as we know it today, was transformed.

Global Companies' plans to build a facility to heat crude oil at the Port of Albany is in the general vicinity of where Albany historian John Wolcott has determined that the original Fort Nassau is located. Wolcott was also responsible for finding the remains of the original Fort Orange in the early 1970s.

It is imperative that a complete archeological excavation takes place on the entire parcel that Global Companies' is proposing. Because of the physical dimensions of the site, the building, stockade, moat and breastworks and the overall size of the Fort, a complete excavations is warranted, not a sample size, or Phase II survey.

The Curtiss "Albany Flyer" in 1910.

A complete excavation of the site is needed to determine if this most important archeological site, and beginning of Albany's (and America's) European history, can be revealed and plans made to preserve as much as possible if the boiling plant is approved.

It is ironic that Fort Nassau would now be newsworthy as it was also in January, four hundred years ago, that Fort Nassau was being built and setting the stage for the Dutch occupation of New York and the beginning of Dutch principles of tolerance and pluralism which make up the foundation of American democracy.

It is also ironic that the celebration of Albany's four hundred anniversary would be marked by its ultimate destruction by an oil boiling plant.

Port of Albany on June 12, 1951.

# The Albany Greenbelt Revisited
First Published on August 22, 2014 at 12:09 am

Back in 1984 I proposed a 30 mile hiking trail around the city of Albany called the Albany Greenbelt. While I mapped the entire route out, with the help of my friends Maria Trabka and Nancy Williams, at the time, the usual Albany politics prevented it from being completed. It's still a good idea and here it is.

Many people have no idea that the political bounds of the city is surrounded by green space. The Hudson River forms the eastern boundary while the Patroon's Creek and Pine Bush form the northern and much of the western boundary and the Normanskill Valley forms the southern boundary

When I was the Albany City Archeologist in the early 1970s, I was amazed at how such an ancient city, founded in 1614, could still have so much original wilderness around its political boundaries after 400 years!! Surely we must preserve it and allow everyone to enjoy it, or so I thought.

Tivoli Hollow Route.

While then Mayor Erastus Corning approved of the project, it never got off the ground. So, when I began working as the Pine Bush Preserve Manager in early 1983 for then Mayor Thomas Whalen, I again proposed the project and this time received his blessing, along with the City Planner and the Parks and Recreation Commissioner.

Even a young new alderman named Jerry Jennings thought it was a great idea.

I worked on the project for two years, and with volunteers Maria Trabka and Nancy Williams, we explored every step of the 30 mile route. This combination of hiking and biking trail encircled the four major natural regions that surround the city and that includes the Hudson River corridor, Patroon's Creek/Tivoli Hollow corridor, the Pine Bush, and the Normanskill Valley. Hikers would walk over many a pristine land if the project had been completed.

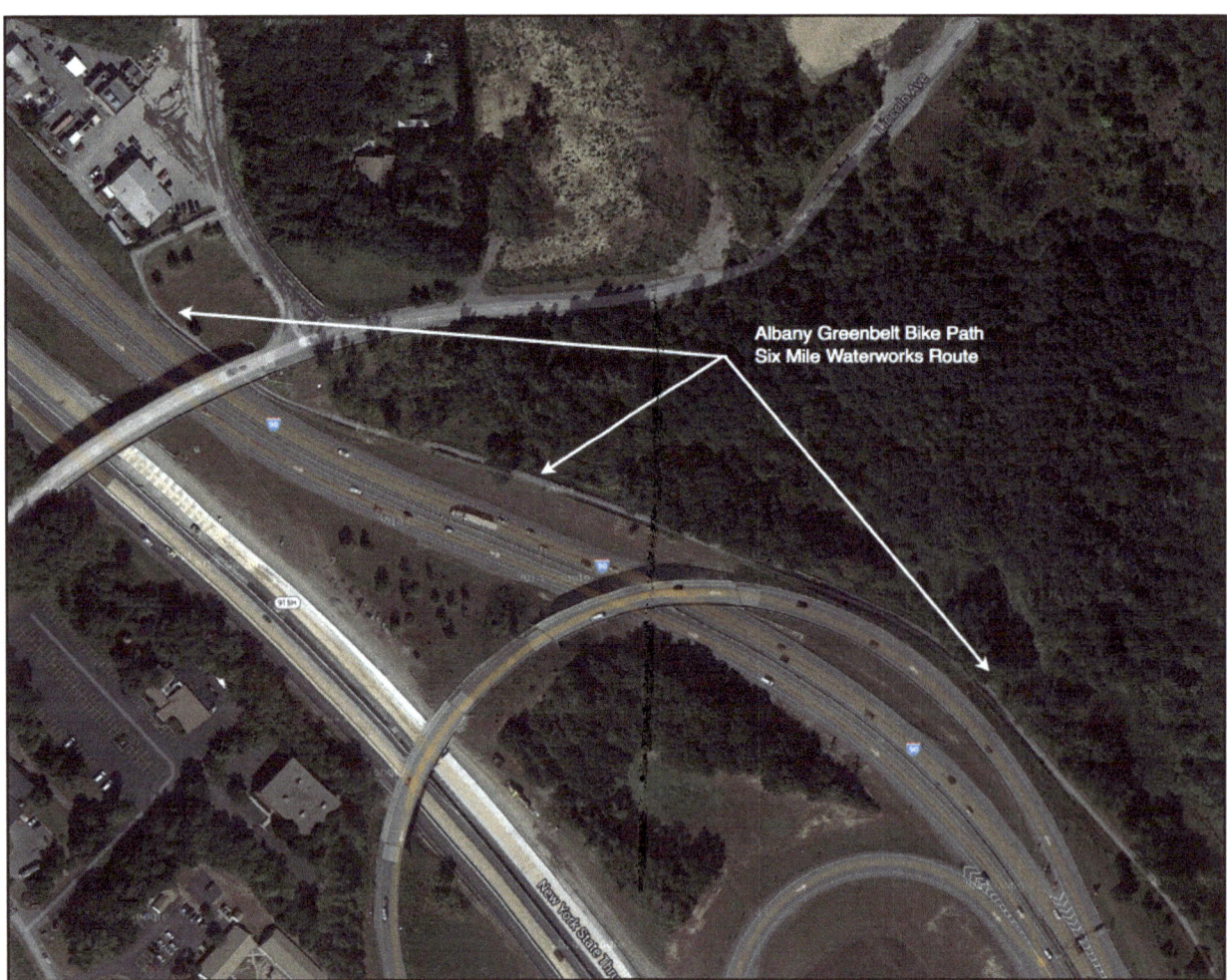

Bike path in Six Mile Waterworks, Albany Greenbelt.

Part of the trail was to be paved for bikes, but most of it was a natural hiking route that was marked with special markers and a guidebook. It also was educational in scope. Hikers would not only explore the natural history of the region but the trail passed many a historic site as well.

In 1984, I met with members of DOT who at the time were redesigning the new Exit 24 interchange. They - in the form of engineer Bill Heilmann - made a commitment to build a paved bike section of the Greenbelt from 6 Mile Waterworks to a section between the Thruway and along the Albany Landfill, about a mile total. It was completed, including a bridge, and exists today (see pictures). The bike trail ends about half way along the landfill, with the hopes that it would eventually be extended.

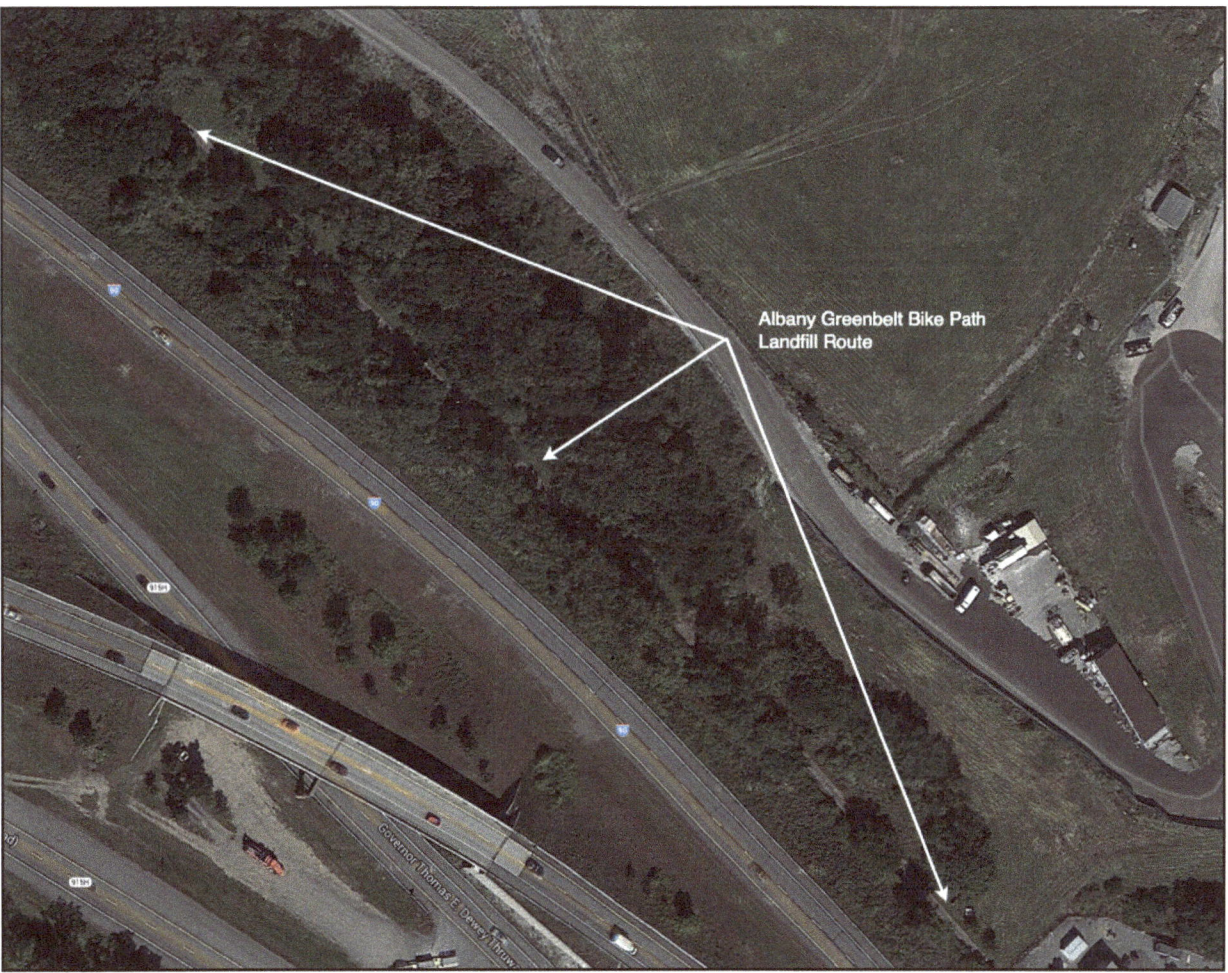

Bike path by landfill. Currently ends about mid way, Albany Greenbelt.

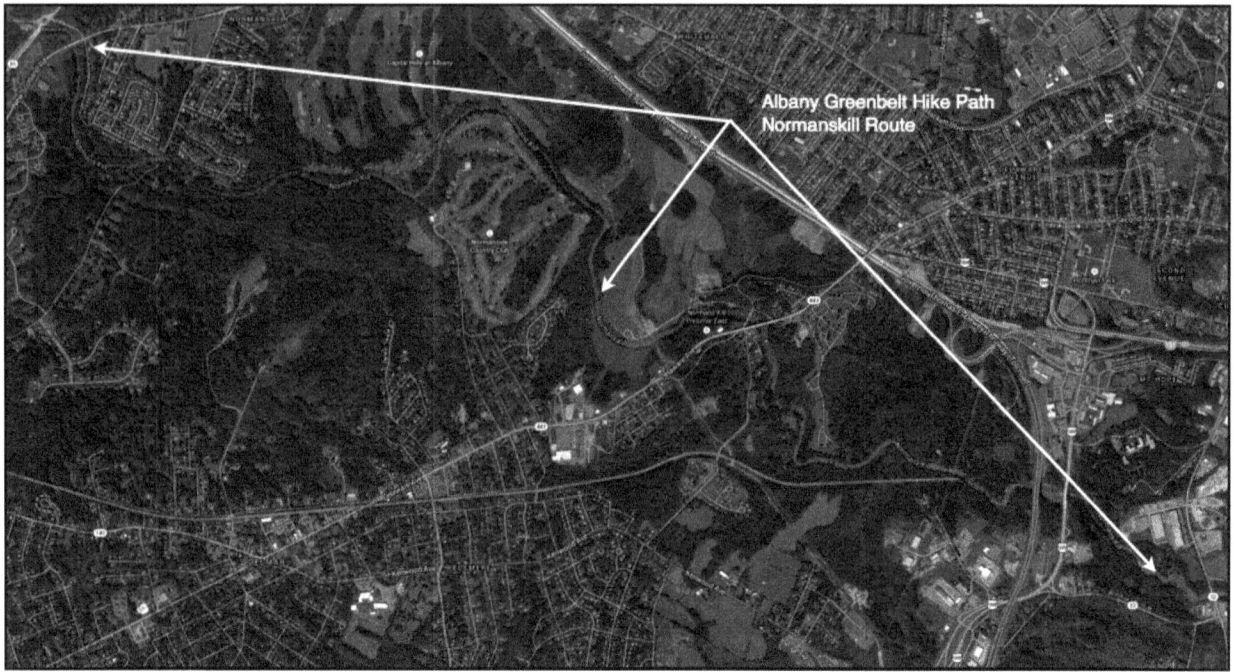

Hike path along the Normanskill, Albany Greenbelt.

The remaining bike route would go up to the Pine Bush preserve and under Route 146 where it would meet with the original King's Highway and other trails until it reached the Normanskill on the western edge of the city. There the city was building a hiking/biking portion of the route down the Normanskill Valley where they were improving the golf range.

I also negotiated with several landowners for easements so hikers could cross their lands. Eventually hikers would find themselves back at the Corning Preserve where it all began.

At the same time I nominated the entire trail system in the city's Pine Bush Preserve as part of the nation's historic recreational trail system, again with Whalen's blessing. In 1985 it became an official part of the National Recreational Trail system. The basic idea was to have this main 30 mile route (Greenbelt) with junctions where hikers or bikers could detour and visit several natural and historic regions that were adjacent to the main Greenbelt route. The King's Highway National Recreational Trail system was a part of the overall Greenbelt design and allowed a hiker or biker to explore the entire Pine Bush Preserve, before he or she continued the longer route. I had a great sign made up for the entrance to the city Pine Bush Preserve and it stood for years until the Pine Bush Commission took it down – I'm not pleased. The day we were going to announce the acceptance into the national trail system was the same day Whalen let me go for being an outspoken critic of development. They cancelled the

Part of the original King's Highway in the Pine Bush was part of the Albany Greenbelt. I erected 26 of these markers in 1975 along the original route.

**EDITORIALS**

**30-mile nature trail**

With a little bit of luck, area residents will soon have a 30-mile hiking and nature trail encircling the city of Albany. The proposed route, known as the Albany Greenbelt, includes glimpses of the area's rich past, a wandering path through the environmentally sensitive Pine Bush and a demanding fitness walk around creeks and abandoned railroad beds.

The trail is the brainchild of Albany Conservation Officer Don Rittner who, along with two associates, has surveyed the entire stretch and planned the connections from one path or walkway to another. When completed — perhaps as early as this summer — the trail will be posted with markers and a book will be available to help guide visitors along.

We wish the designers of the trail the best of luck on this extremely worthy contribution to local history and the out-of-doors. When all the necessary rights of way have finally been secured, the trail will provide handsome grounds for hiking, jogging, cross country skiing, and, in certain sections, bicycling.

Besides disclosing nature's beauty, the trail will also give users a glimpse at some local history that has, for the most part, remained hidden. The seldom seen sights will include the Tivoli Lakes nature sanctuary, which used to be the water supply for the city, and the original Erie Canal and lumber district of Albany, now filled with a road, Erie Boulevard. Traces of the canal path on which horses pulled the barges can still be seen along Erie Boulevard and will serve as part of the new bike and hiking path.

The path, which will cost little, promises to provide unlimited pleasure to area residents. We look forward to its opening.

press conference and to this day the city has never announced it.

There was a great deal of media exposure about the project at the time. Of course Albany politics stepped its ugly head in the end and the project was never completed.

The Albany Greenbelt is still a good idea. Certainly biking trails are accepted without question now — they were just starting when we proposed the Greenbelt. Most of the connections are still there. There is much more of the Pine Bush preserved and available and the Normanskill is still relatively untouched. I won't hold my breath.

1984 Editorial in the Times Union supporting the Albany Greenbelt.

Part of the original King's Highway in the Pine Bush was part of the Albany Greenbelt. I erected 26 of these markers in 1975 along the original route. The Pine Bush Commission took it down.

The Albany Greenbelt goes through much of the unique Pine Bush.

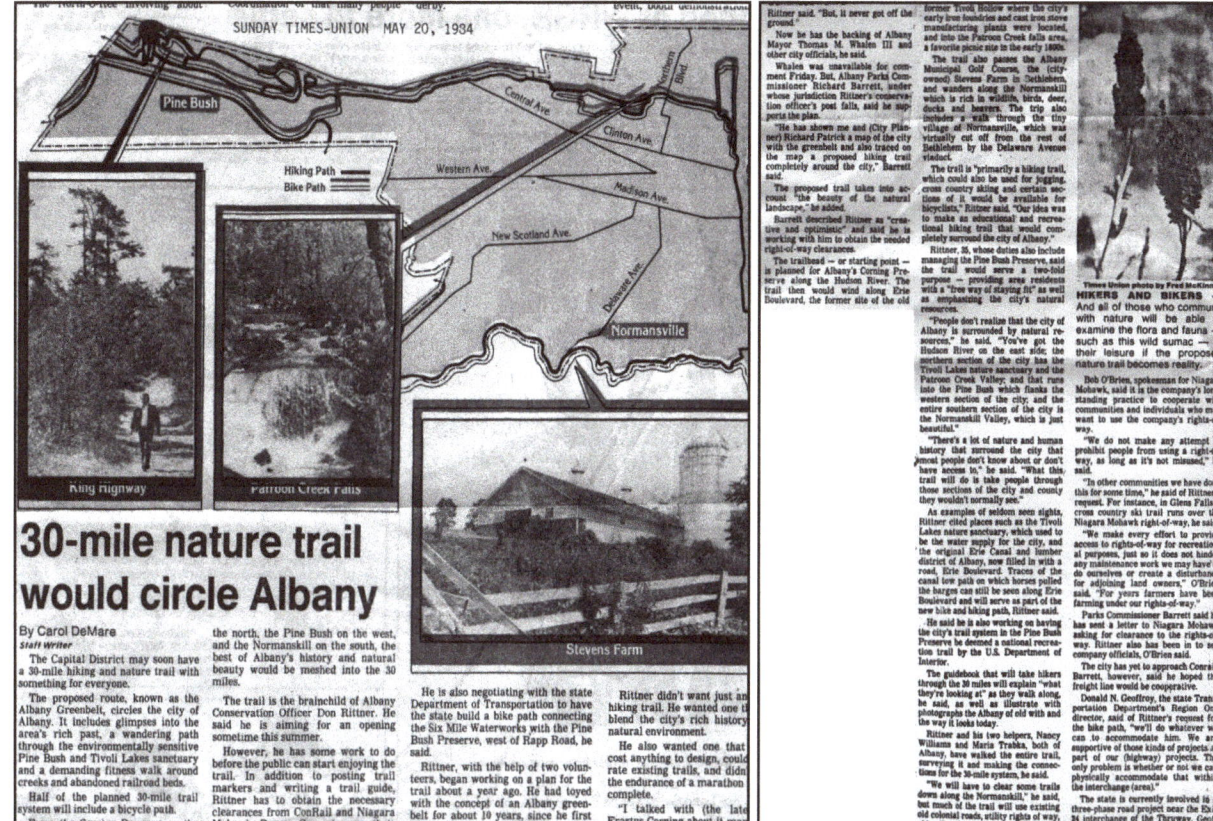
Times Union article by Carole Demare on the Albany Greenbelt on May 20, 1984.

The Albany Greenbelt is for young and old.

Aerial view of the Port of Albany. A few boats appear to be loading at the docks along the river. Storage tanks are clustered on both sides of the river. In the background, three bridges connect the cities of Albany on the left and Rensselaer on the right. 1937. New York State Archives. Education Dept. Division of Visual Instruction. Instructional lantern slides, 1911-1925, A3045-78, Lantern slide DnAkY7.

# North Dakota's Crude Trick on Albany

First published on January 19, 2014 1:17 am

There is a lot of talk and interest regarding the proposal to build a heating facility at the Port of Albany as it relates to the handling of what may be North Dakota crude oil or oil from Canada.

Albany has now become an important point in the route of this highly volatile and toxic crude oil from North Dakota and other points. From the Port of Albany the oil is transported via tankers down the Hudson River and on to refineries.

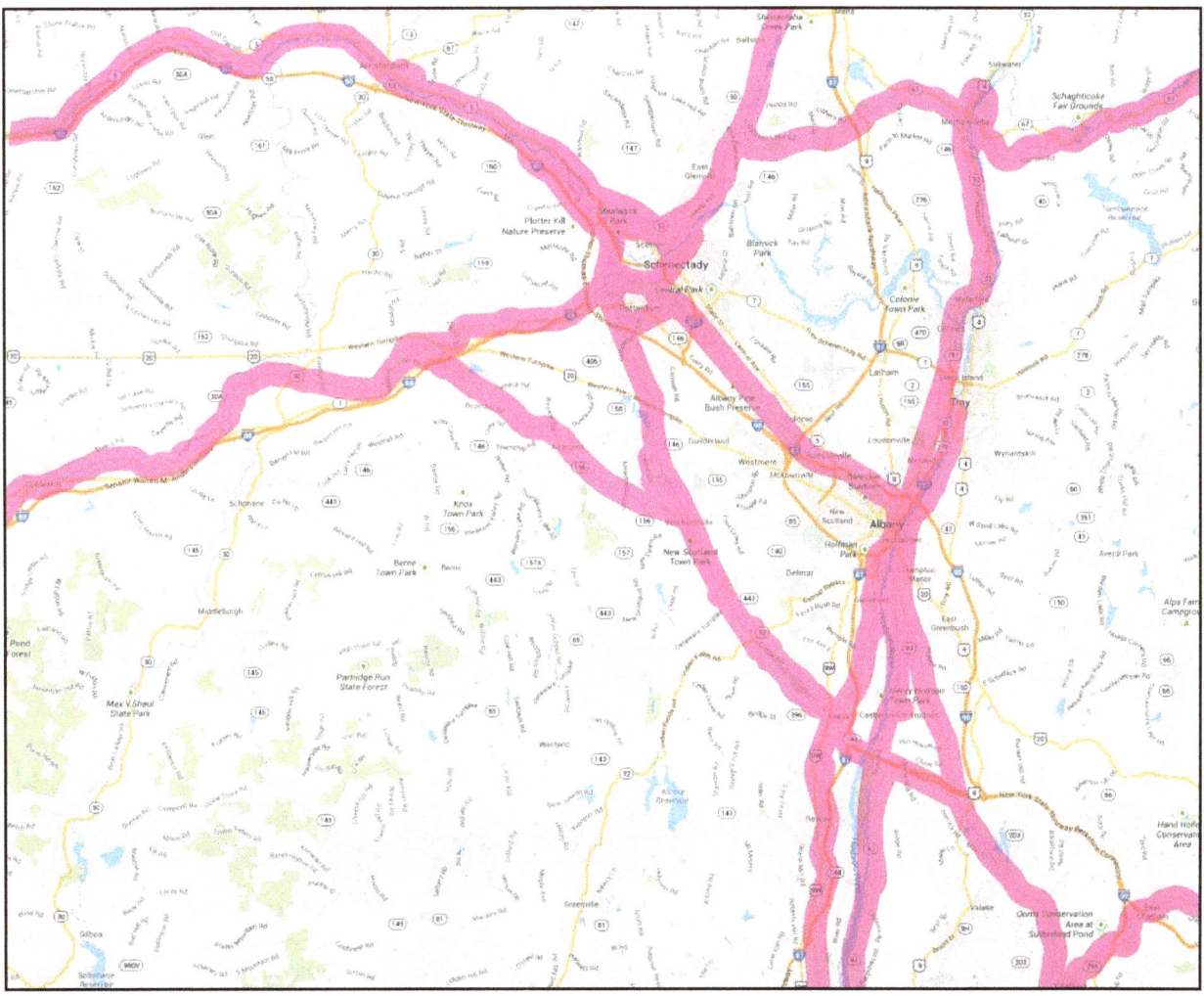

Impact locations if we have a similar rail derailment as July's Canada accident. Prepared by Andy Arthur.

New York's Department of Environmental Conservation has approved one company's ability to double the amount shipped here and that could mean a billion gallons every year.

The Massachusetts company, Global Partners, wants to build a heating facility at the port so it can make its thick tar-like oil less thick so it can flow into tankers. There was a 50% increase in the country in rail shipments of this oil and other products during the first half of 2013. The number of accidents also increased to almost 150 during the year.

The runaway train carrying Bakken formation crude oil in July that exploded in Lac Magnatic Quebec killed 47 people, destroyed half of the downtown, and could happen here with greater results. Andy Arthur prepared a map that shows which areas would be affected in the Capital District, based on rail locations, if a similar accident

1639 Vingboom Map showing location of Fort Nassau and Fort Orange. Castle Island is now the Port of Albany. LOC.

occurred. In some areas like Schenectady, kiss it goodbye! Drive down the port and look at the oil cars sitting next to the low-income housing projects. Talk about a disaster waiting to happen?

However, with all that said about the environmental issues, there is another concern regarding local and important history.

Global Partners wants to place this heating facility on the site of Fort Nassau, the site of the very first location of European occupation in 1614 that became Albany. Around this time in January, 400 years ago, a Dutch ship called the *Fortyne* (Fortune) sailed to the forested Castle Island (now Port of Albany) and built a small fort to trade with the local Native American population (Mohicans).

Under the command of Hendrick Christaensen, his sailors built a small fort with permission of the local Mohican Nation. Local historian John Wolcott knows where the site is and it is in the general area where they want to build the heating facility.

I have known Wolcott for 40 years. He is one of the best researchers I have ever known and I would put money in the bank anytime he told me where a site is. He also knew where Fort Orange was located in the early 1970s and that was partially excavated because of his research and then, unfortunately, the State of New York covered it over with a ramp for the newly created I-787 road system. Wolcott has found that Fort Nassau may have been larger than the later Fort Orange. The fort on the island itself was 58 feet across within the quadrangle but it had an 18 foot moat around it so there is likely remains waiting to be discovered.

Under normal circumstances, an archeological excavation would be required before this heating facility could be built. Albany has it in City code that the position of City Archeologist has to review a site and this position has been funded in the previous City budgets to the tune of several thousand dollars.

Yet, Albany hasn't had a City Archeologist on the payroll in years even though it had the payroll allocated. That means there was no one watching the store. No archeologist to review the mandated archeological review of many projects that were approved and built in the city without archeology even being done, and no archeologist on staff to review the archeological reports when they were actually done.

I reviewed the last three that were submitted to the city (I was the first city archeologist in the country in 1973 to 1979 when I worked for the late Erastus Corning) as a courtesy and found them lacking.

One development, the Paul Clark Tavern site, at the corner of Madison and Lark, has been held up after the fact. The building was torn down and then an archeological review was mandated only to find structures that should have been known BEFORE the building was taken down. Everything was done wrong on this project. Frankly, I am surprised the city has not been sued.

The site of Fort Nassau is of utmost importance as it is the first Dutch built building in North America (actually first European structure). It is the beginning of the Dutch occupation in America that gave rise to what it means to be an American today; the principles of pluralism and tolerance and much of our legal system. I would consider this site one of the most important in New York State and the United States. I am sure the Dutch government will also be interested in this site.

So here is the irony. The year 2014 is the 400 year anniversary of the founding of Albany and the site of this historic beginning, one of the most important archeological sites in North America, will likely be covered over by an oil heating facility for crude oil.

Nice anniversary present.

Happy 400th Albany.

# Boiling Plant Should be Designed for any Possibility

First published on January 30, 2014 at 8:42 am

I was thinking "what if" lately. What if the oil boiling facility proposed by Global Companies gets built at the Port of Albany. There has been a great deal discussed about possible explosions, which is certainly possible, but what other problems could occur that would have a possible negative effect on the plant being there.

The Port has had some problems in the past. In 1958, the Grange League Federation mill exploded and burned on March 3rd and took two lives and injured 21 workers. In 1960, Sears Oil was charged with polluting the Hudson when they were accused of discharging oil into the river. On November 17th, 1962 a spark from the ignition of a nearby car caused an explosion at the Mobile Oil Co. plant. Two men were hurt with severe burns. None of the nearby oil tanks caught on fire but the fire happened right outside a four and one half million gallon tank.

On September 8th, 1980 a large fire erupted in the gasoline storage area and set off two large explosions with mushroom balls of flame from two tanks owned by Mobile Oil. Over 1000 people had to be evacuated. Eight persons, seven of them firemen, were injured and one fireman seriously. For 3 ½ hours residents along South Pearl Street near the port had to leave their homes and part of Interstate 787 was closed, and two exits from the thruway. The coast guard closed the river to all traffic.

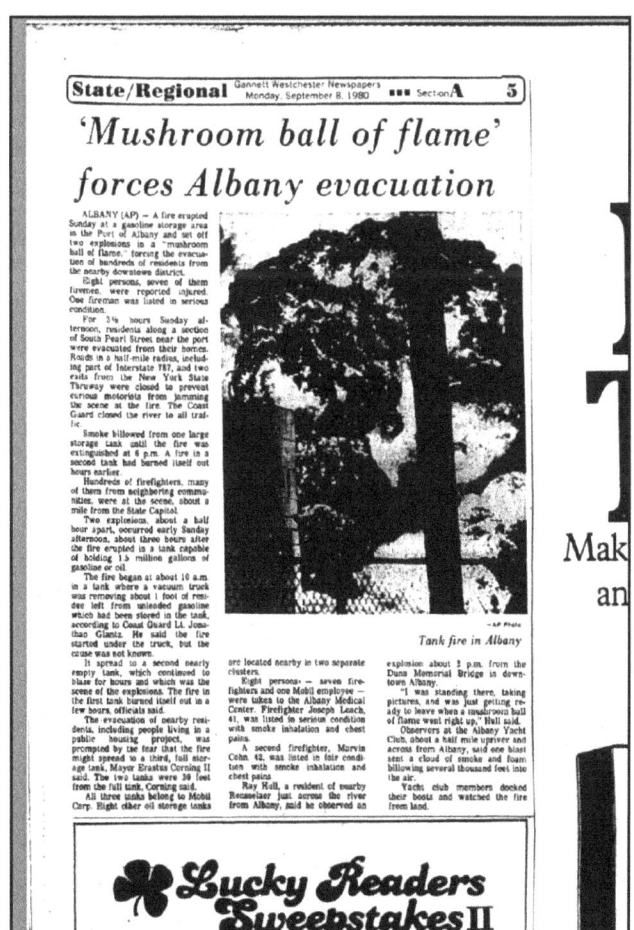

September 8, 1980, tank explosion in Albany evacuated 1000 residents.

Another concern is the location of seismic fault lines in the Capital District. What would happen if there was an earthquake greater than 5.0? According to geologists there have been a number of unexplainable as of yet series of small quakes in Albany County in the Berne area in 2011. This is what the

NYS Museum describes:

*"The Albany, New York area experienced 24 small, deep earthquakes between Monday, August 22 and Sunday, August 28. These minor earthquakes occurred below the Helderberg plateau in the Town of Knox, approximately 12 miles west of Albany. The earthquakes had magnitudes of 1.6 to 2.9, and occurred at depths of 17.6 to 24.0 kilometers (10.9 to 14.9 miles).*

*Earthquake ("seismic") records for the region, available beginning in the late 1970s, indicate an unusual number of small, deep earthquakes occur in the Helderbergs. Between 1980 and 2007, 30 earthquakes were recorded beneath the Town of Berne, immediately south of Knox. Between February 2009 and March 2010, 37 additional earthquakes occurred below Berne. The Berne earthquakes had magnitudes between 1.1 to 3.1, and occurred at depths of 4-22 kilometers (2.5 to 13.7 miles).*

*The latest series of 24 earthquakes represent the first recorded earthquakes in Knox.*

*Earthquakes generally occur when there is sudden movement along a break in rocks, called a fault. Earthquakes with a magnitude of 2.0 to 2.9 or less are generally not felt; those between 3.0-3.9 are more commonly felt, but rarely cause damage.*

*The pattern of earthquake activity in the Helderbergs west of Albany points to small amounts of slip along deeply-buried faults. The rocks at those depths are over a billion years old, and are seen exposed in the Adirondack Mountains to the north. Two known fault zones extend toward the Helderbergs from the southern Adirondacks and the Saratoga-Ballston Spa area. Bedrock mapping in the Helderbergs has not found any significant faults that reach the surface; vertical faults found in the Helderbergs so far show only a vertical slip of a few tens of centimeters (up to one to two feet), and could have formed anytime from recently to hundreds of millions of years ago.*

*In and around New York, most earthquakes occur in the area of the central to northern Adirondacks and adjacent parts of Quebec and Ontario, or in the greater New York City area. The reason for such a concentration of earthquakes deep below the Helderbergs is not known, and is catching the attention of seismologists, geologists who specialize in the study of earthquakes."*

It's that last sentence, *"Catching the attention of seismologists"* that gets *my* attention. It may be nothing at all?

Basically they do not know what is causing them nor the extent to what will happen in the future. This series of quakes called a swarm may have been related to an event in Virginia at the same time. There is a fault system near us called the Saratoga-

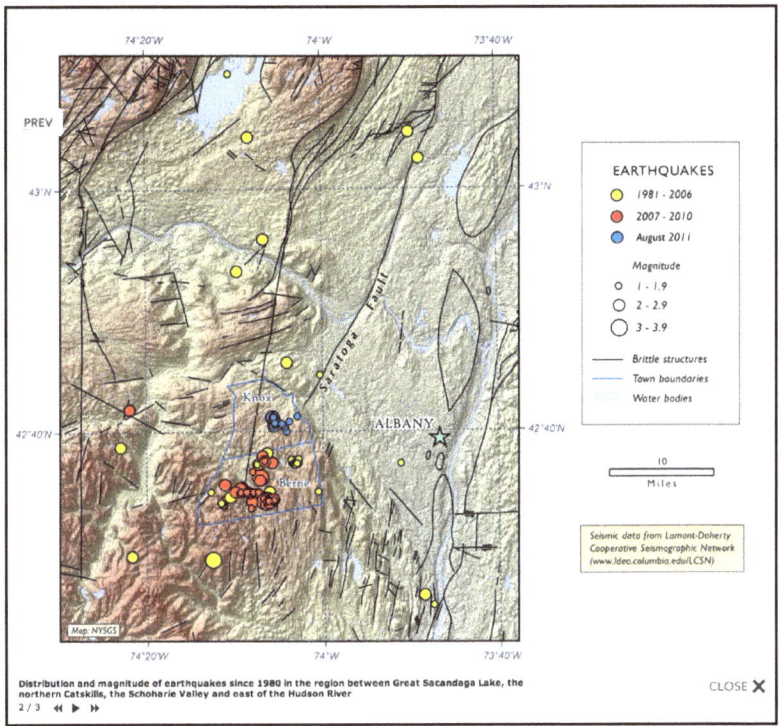

Fault Hazards. Brittle Structure.

McGregor Fault System. A scientific report published by the Geological Society of America said:

*"The Saratoga-McGregor fault has been mapped to the north, where it brings Precambrian against Ordovician units, and has been presumed to be primarily a Taconic aged fault with down drop to the east on the order of 150 m for Ordovician horizons, with a possible strike slip component. Other "Mohawk Valley faults," for which we have seismic reflection data, were active in Iapetan opening time, and were reactivated in the Taconic, Salinic, (neo) Acadian/Alleghanian, and some presently experience limited seismicity. If the 2011 earthquake swarm is related to the Mineral VA seismic event, then the 2011 earthquake swarm indicates that the S-M fault sustained a stress release in response to the same stress (and release) that faults at Mineral experienced. It might be that the S-M fault was active during Triassic/Jurassic rifting—the structural location of the S-M fault indicates the fault could well have experienced minor activity during Triassic/Jurassic rifting, in which case the S-M fault is in a somewhat similar structural setting to the activated fault(s) at Mineral VA."*

I am not sure what that all means but if an earthquake in Virginia causes movement up here, I would be interested in it.

Another geological map that shows the number of quakes from 1981 to present also shows the areas of "Brittle Structures," something I read as areas that could break, fracture or fault. There seems to be two circular areas around the Port area on the map.

A USGS map shows us somewhat near the middle of a major earthquake hazard risk.

Of course there is also the possibility of flooding. What impact would that have on the boiling plant site? Certainly the floods of 1913 and 1936 covered the entire port.

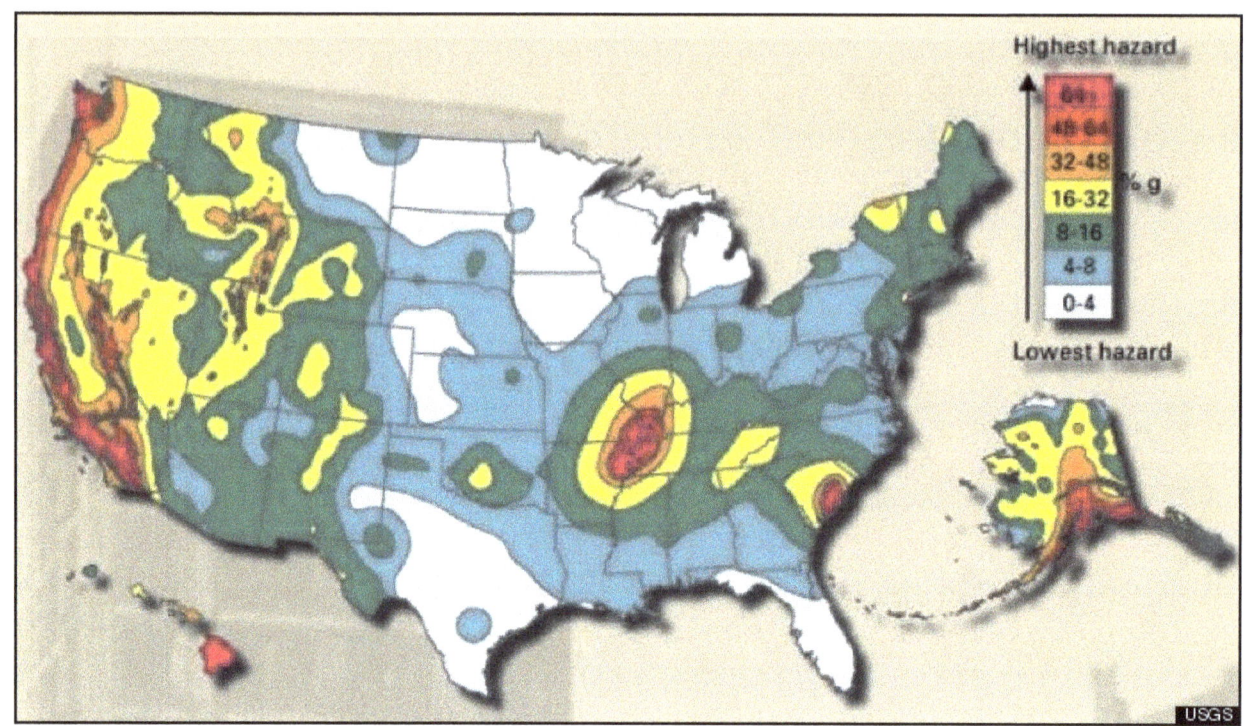

Albany is close to the middle of potential hazards from an earthquake. From the Net.

Could another flood happen and what would it do to the boiling facility and the cars

The Port area under water during a 1936 flood in Albany.

Albany's Broadway in 1913.

stored there with potential explosive oil?

The entire South End was uninhabitable during the March 1913 flood.

There is the whole subject of sea level rising. Certainly the Port would be under water if the river rose. It is in the 100 year flood zone already but climatologists are predicting sea level rise is on the rise. What does that mean for our area?

In 1963 the Port was approved for the shipping of nuclear materials. Is that still valid? Are their nuclear materials still being taken in or out of the Port and what safety precautions are being taken? What could happen if there were nuclear

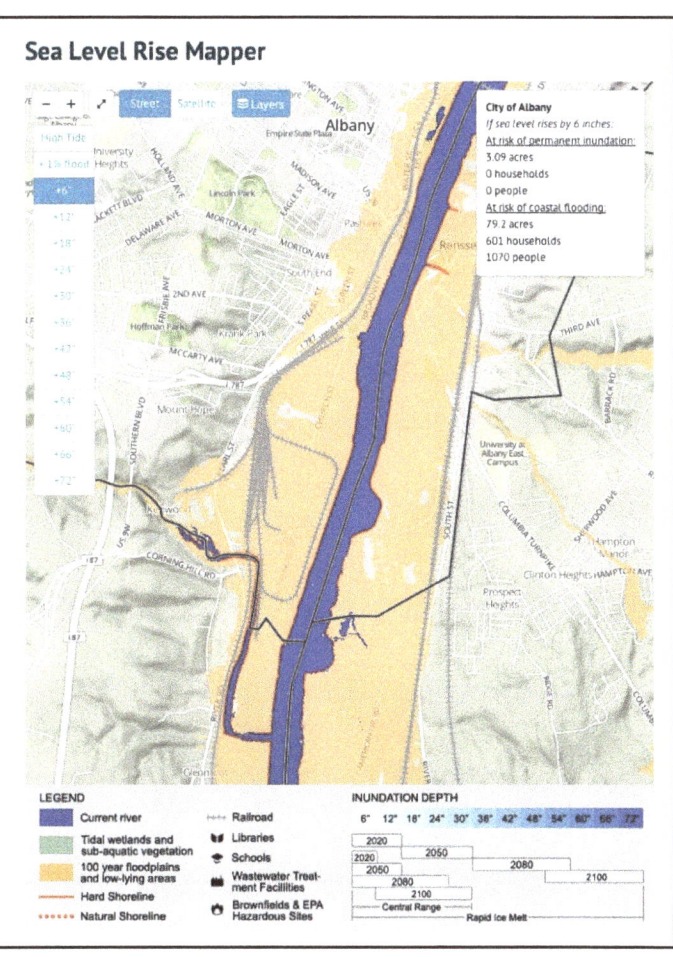

Sea level rise could affect the Port area. From the Net.

materials being stored and the boiling plant exploded? The problems with Nuclear Lead in Colonie in the 1980s come to mind.

I think it is safe to say overall the Port of Albany has a good record of safety but it would seem prudent that all these factors be considered if the boiling plant is approved and that these possibilities are part of the design of the plant.

What if?

Better to be safe than sorry.

One of the largest environmental cleanups in Capital Region history was National Lead. The federal government is trying to auction off the former National Lead factory site on Central Avenue. The contaminant of greatest concern is depleted uranium, not lead. The facility at the Albany border was contaminated with microscopic particles of depleted uranium (DU) to the extent that former employees were still excreting it in their urine 30-plus years after shutdown. This is a cartoon we did in 1982. They closed in 1984 from a court order.

# Preserve Fort Nassau, and Fort Nassau 2, and Fort Nassau 3, and………

First published on August 15, 2014 10:10 pm

This year marks the 400th anniversary of the beginning of Albany. In the spring of 1614 a Dutch ship called the Fortune landed on an island called Castle Island (now Port of Albany) and erected a small fort called Fort Nassau. Here was erected a trading house 38 by 27 feet, a defensive wall (either palisade or horizontal wall) 58 by 58 foot square and was surrounded by an 18 foot moat. The outpost was named after Prince Maurice, the Prince of Orange/Nassau in the Netherlands. This was the only Dutch "occupation" with a building in North America. They later built Fort Orange on the mainland and the rest is Albany history.

And so the story goes…

Unfortunately for historians and archeologists there is more to the story. In fact there may have been more than one fort built on the island.

Block's Map of 1614 shows the location of Fort Nassau but a smudge on the map makes it hard to see.

Captain Adriaen Block was in charge of the trading expedition in 1613 that began in New York Bay. Block had to build a ship there called the Onrust because his ship the

Tyger burned over the winter. Block sent skipper Hendrick Christiaenson up the Hudson with his ship the Fortune to build Fort Nassau and he made a very good figurative map of his explorations when he returned to the Netherlands the same year, 1614.

On the original map that is available at the Hague there is a smudge on the island that makes it hard to see the location of the fort. Fortunately someone made an exact reproduction of it and you can see the dot that locates the fort on the southern part of the island and on the western side of the island where the Normanskill meets Island Creek, the creek that really is part of the Hudson River. Problem is the Normanskill is not on the map. Why? Well, Block was on a voyage to create a trading network with the local Native population to trade for furs and make money. He and everyone else knew that it was a lucrative field in the new world. He obviously had permission to build Fort Nassau from the local Mohicans who controlled both sides of the Hudson at the time but further west was the rich fur lands of the Iroquois and it just so happens that the Normanskill begins up there in Schenectady County not far from the Mohawk River and the source of all those furs. Why put that important corridor on a map so your competitors could see it? Even then you needed to keep your cards close to the vest.

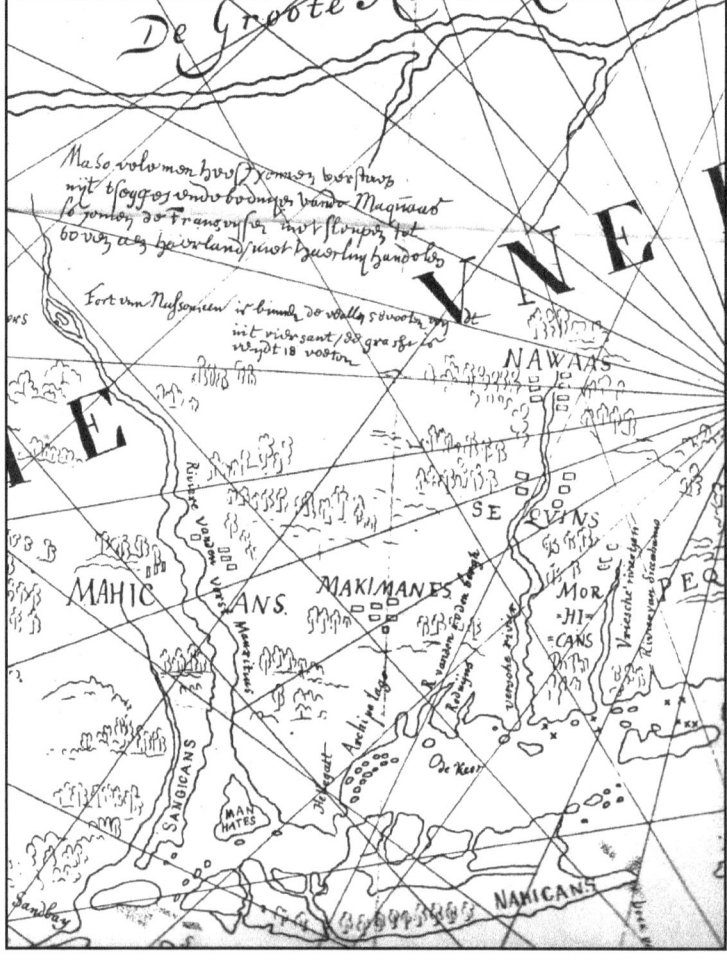

Section of 1848 hand drawn copy of the 1614 Block map showing Ft. Nassau near confluence of Normanskill (not shown). Supplied by John Wolcott.

Historians have written that Fort Nassau was flooded and eventually moved to the mainland and Fort Orange was built, to replace it, but not so fast. There is no doubt that the island kept getting flooded. Let's put it this way. The Normanskill drains over 40 miles of land through Schenectady and Albany Counties with a drainage basin of 170 square miles. That's a lot of water. The last mile is tidal.

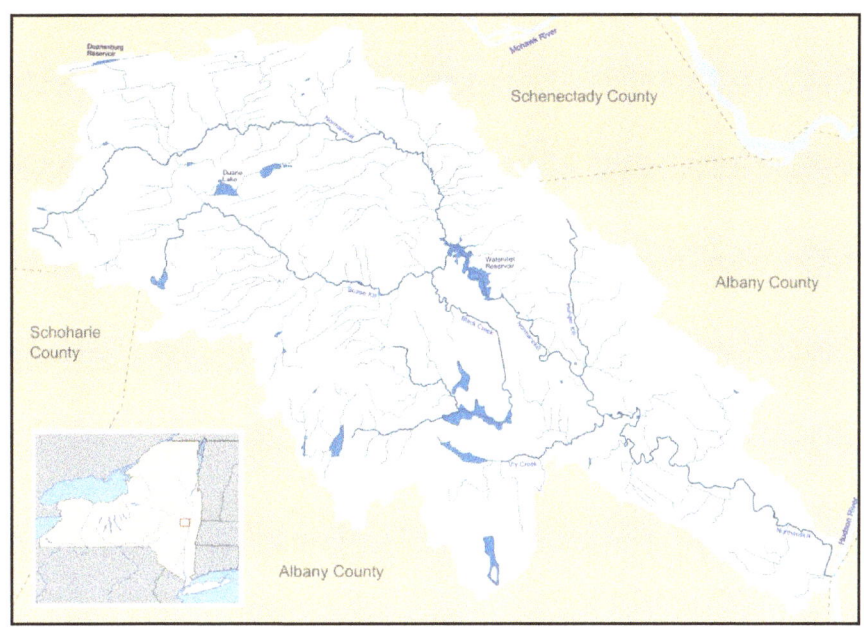

The drainage of the Normanskill is huge and empties out from a small 100 foot wide outlet into Island Creek. Map from the Internet.

The average discharge today is 150 cu ft./s. You bet it flooded Castle Island probably each year.

So you can assume after the first year of Fort Nassau being across from the Normanskill and getting flooded someone thought it might be a good idea to move away from it. That brings up another map.

Before Block went back to the Netherlands in 1614 he handed over the Onrust to Cornelius Hendrickson who spent the next two years exploring the Delaware Bay and he also produced a map. However on his map Fort Nassau was located somewhat in the middle and bit north on the island. Logical when you consider that if the fort was flooded since it was built (in 1614) that two years later when he made his map he would have placed the fort where he knew it was — then relocated in the middle of the island. Follow the logic? So far everything seems fine. The original fort was built near a fresh water stream as most forts of the time were (If there were no streams they would have a well or spring, i.e., Dongan Fort in Schenectady). It was flooded

The Onrust (Dutch for Restless) under the command of Adriaen Block visited Castle Island in 1614 to check on the progress of the building of Fort Nassau. Photo by Linda Bobar.

Hendrickson's Map of 1616, two years after Block, shows Fort Nassau more in the middle of the island.

so logic would dictate you rebuild it where you don't get wet. They certainly were not here long enough to know the geology and hydrology of the region.

Let's fast forward a few years to another map known as the Vingboom Map of 1639 although Albany historian John Wolcott gives an earlier date of around 1626-27 for this map. On this map it shows now on the mainland Fort Orange that was built in 1624 but the ruins of another fort, perhaps Fort Nassau 3, on the northern tip of the island. Or could this be Fort Orange 1?

Confused yet?

We have as evidence the Block and Hendrickson Maps of 1614 and 1616, arguably first hand accounts of the locations of Fort Nassau across from the Normanskill and in the middle of the island. Then there is this third location at the north of the island.

Early Dutch writers who we can rely on somewhat since they were close to the time period are Nicholaes Van

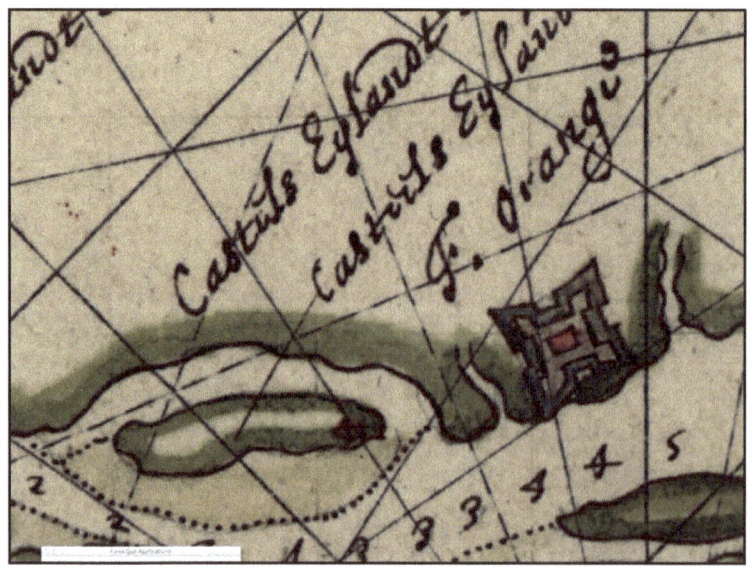

The Vingboom Map shows both Fort Nassau, location 3, and Fort Orange on the mainland.

116

Wassnaer writing in 1624 and Johan De Laet in 1625. Neither was in the area but had access probably to Block's journals, word of mouth, and other resources.

Wassenaer in his "Historisch Verhael" wrote that Fort Nassau was built *"on an island in 42 degrees on the north side of the River Montagne, now called Mauritius."* Whoops that does not jive with any of the maps referred to earlier? He also goes on to say that the Dutch had built Fort Orange with Four Bastions *"on an island, by them called Castle Island."* Even Simon Hart who wrote the History of the New Netherland Company mentioned Fort Orange on Castle Island but not in context? Archeology that was done on Fort Orange in the early 1970s by Paul Huey partially excavated Fort Orange and it was not on Castle Island. According to historian Wolcott Huey proclaimed in the newspaper that he had enough info and they built the 1787 ramp on top of it. Well, looks like that may not have been true.

Wassenaer also wrote about natives from the interior coming down the river to trade and *"great quantities of water running to the river, overflowing the adjoining country, which was the cause that Fort Nassau was frequently lay under water and was abandoned."*

We do know that some of that is true. David De Vries who did visit the area in 1639 was visiting friends who lived on Castle Island. On January 30, 1639, while at Fort Orange *"there came such a flood upon the island on which Brand Pijlen dwelt [my host for the time being], that we had to abandon the island, and to use boats in going to the house, for the water stood about four feet deep on the island, whereas the latter lies seven or eight feet above ordinary water. This high water lasted three days before we could use the houses again. The water came into the fort. We had to resort to the woods, where we set up tents and kept great fires going."*

A few years later in 1680 Jasper Dankers and Peter Sluyter in their journal on Sunday, January 28th writes: *"in the afternoon, we took a walk to an island upon the end of which there is a fort built, they say by the Spaniards. That a fort has been there is evident enough from the earth thrown up and strewn round, but it is not to be supposed that the Spaniards came so far inland to built forts, when there are no monuments of them to be seen elsewhere and down on the sea coasts, where, however, they have been according to the traditions of the Indians. This fort is a short hour's distance below Albany, on the west side of the river."*

The West side of the river and on the end of the island suggests that they saw the first Fort Nassau?

So in summary, Fort Nassau was built near the confluence of the Normanskill, moved to the middle of the island, and then to the North end of the island where it may have been renamed Fort Orange before they moved over the mainland and built the final Fort Orange.

The only way to prove any of this is to conduct archeological excavations. We almost lost Fort Nassau #3 recently to the proposed Global Companies oil heating plant. We know where to dig! All three sites are available for testing.

This is the beginning of Albany history and it deserves to be thoroughly investigated.

Addendum
My colleague John Wolcott has pin pointed Fort Nassau #3. Read it here:

https://www.newyorkalmanack.com/2014/08/researcher-pinpoints-1614-albany-fort-location/

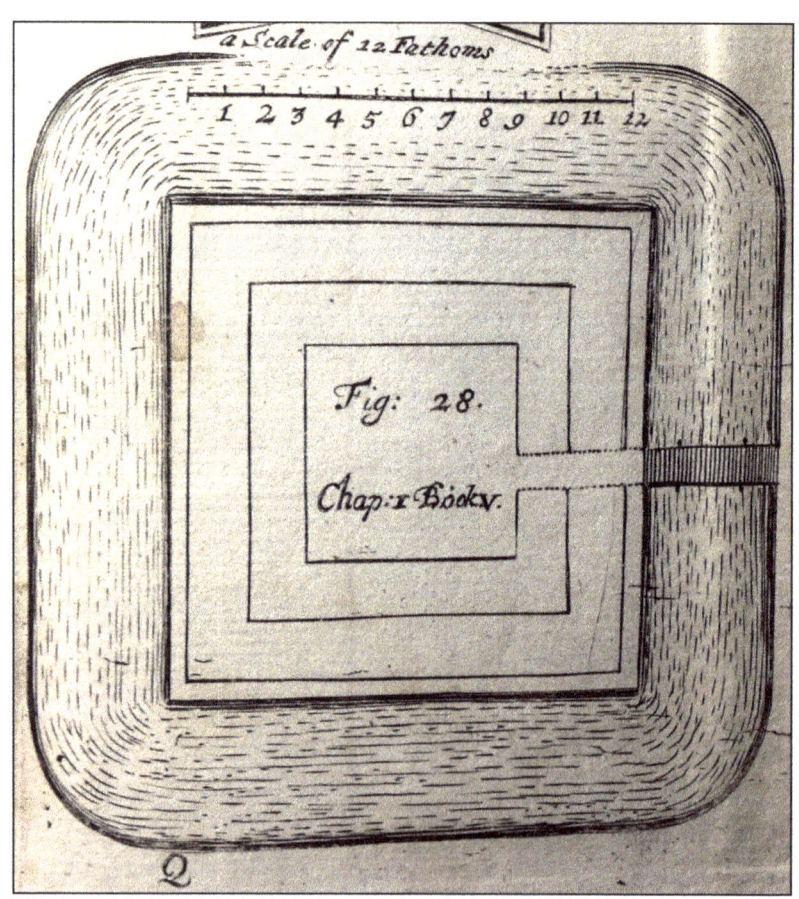

Possible map of Fort Nassau.

# Will the Real Fort Nassau Please Stand Up!
Originally published on October 18, 2014 12:38 am

So it looks like artist Len Tantillo and company want to start a fight! He was quoted in the Schenectady Gazette recently that he wanted to "debunk" John Wolcott's assertions (and mine) of where Fort Nassau is based on his "research" and 3D modeling. Sorry Mr. Tantillo at least Paul Huey has put a trowel in the ground. Like many I appreciate his artistic talents. He has a real knack for creating atmosphere in his works that bring out the real sense and mood of his subjects. So I'm not out to embarrass anyone or cast stones but if you want to debunk a historian like Wolcott who has been doing this for 60 years you better have your pencils and trowels sharpened.

Unfortunately for Mr. Tantillo I do a lot of research too. His first painted interpretation of Fort Orange with vertical post/stockades around it was wrong when the archeology way back in 1970-71 showed it had horizontal posts (see http://www.lftantillo.com/shop/17th-Century/Fort-Orange-1635/prod_65.html). That dig was under the supervision of Paul Huey who then made his career as an archeologist over that excavation, which by the way was only made possible because the site was located precisely by the same John Wolcott that Tantillo wants to "debunk." Also he seems to be going against his friend Huey who has agreed with Wolcott where he is mentioned in the *Atlas of Dutch America*, an ongoing project to find Dutch presence in North America: *"The suggestion by Paul Huey of the fort being near Island Creek Park should be verified."* Island Creek Park is near where Wolcott locates the fort. Huey should make his ideas public. Does he agree or not with Wolcott, his mentor. Or is he now wrong about his earlier assumption? Has the artist trumped the archeologist?

See
http://www.newhollandfoundation.nl/teksten/Report%20Identification%20Mission%20ADNA,%202012.pdf

Be sure to read the footnote that Huey had a hand in the writing.

I have seen four renditions of Fort Nassau by Tantillo - all different. The one used on a recent brochure didn't have a chimney. Must have been pretty smoky? Got to give him credit for at least trying to figure it out. One of his drawings, as shown in Shirley's Dun's *Mohicans and their Land,* show it placed on the southern tip of the island across from the Normanskill, the location that I favor. However in the same book Dunn has it on the North end of the island with the Vingbooms Map. That supports at least two positions and Wolcott's findings on the northern part of the island. Mrs. Dunn should also make her opinions known on the matter. She is an excellent researcher and should join in the debate.

One of Tantillo's early paintings or drawings of Fort Nassau, based on his 3D modeling and research I guess, didn't seem to have a moat around it even though the entire description of the site was printed on a map that was made four centuries ago (see http://www.lftantillo.com/shop/17th-Century/The-Trading-House/prod_63.html). He now claims he knows what it looks like and where it is located based on his latest painting, which I will discuss in a minute.

His painting of early Schenectady with the Dutch Church was wrong also as he painted houses next to it where there should have been headstones (See http://www.lftantillo.com/shop/17th-Century/Schenectady-Town/prod_55.html). The painting taken from an angle that shows Van Velson's mill and the Cowhorn Creek with the Dutch Church in the middle and a row of houses on the left is inaccurate. Any good historian knows that the church cemetery was located there until the first quarter of the 18th century and was later extended. The cemetery was west of the church and was fifteen feet wide and fifty-six feet long. It was enlarged south to 84 feet towards Cowhorn Creek, the rear line being 44 ½ feet. Also Cowhorn Creek actually extends further down past the mill before it bends to the left. Ok, I'm nitpicking about historical accuracy, and an artist does have a certain amount of license — just don't brag about historical accuracy. But he should leave archeology to the archeologists. He later modified his Fort Orange painting when Wolcott informed him of the horizontal posts. He modified his Fort Nassau painting also adding the moat. The Schenectady painting remains as is and has not been modified.

This does not take away from the beauty of his paintings. They are what they are. I give full artistic license to anyone trying to recreate the historical settings of our area, however he is the one that promotes his research abilities and wants to "debunk" Wolcott's research (and mine by association). If folks think they are going to "debunk" John Wolcott they are going to have to put boots on the ground, so to speak, and gather up a whole lot of knowledge about Albany in a hurry. They can bring all the expert archeologists from the Netherlands or Brazil over here that they want. Unless they have been studying this area for the last 60 years, as Wolcott has, their PhDs are meaningless.

I still have my money on Wolcott.

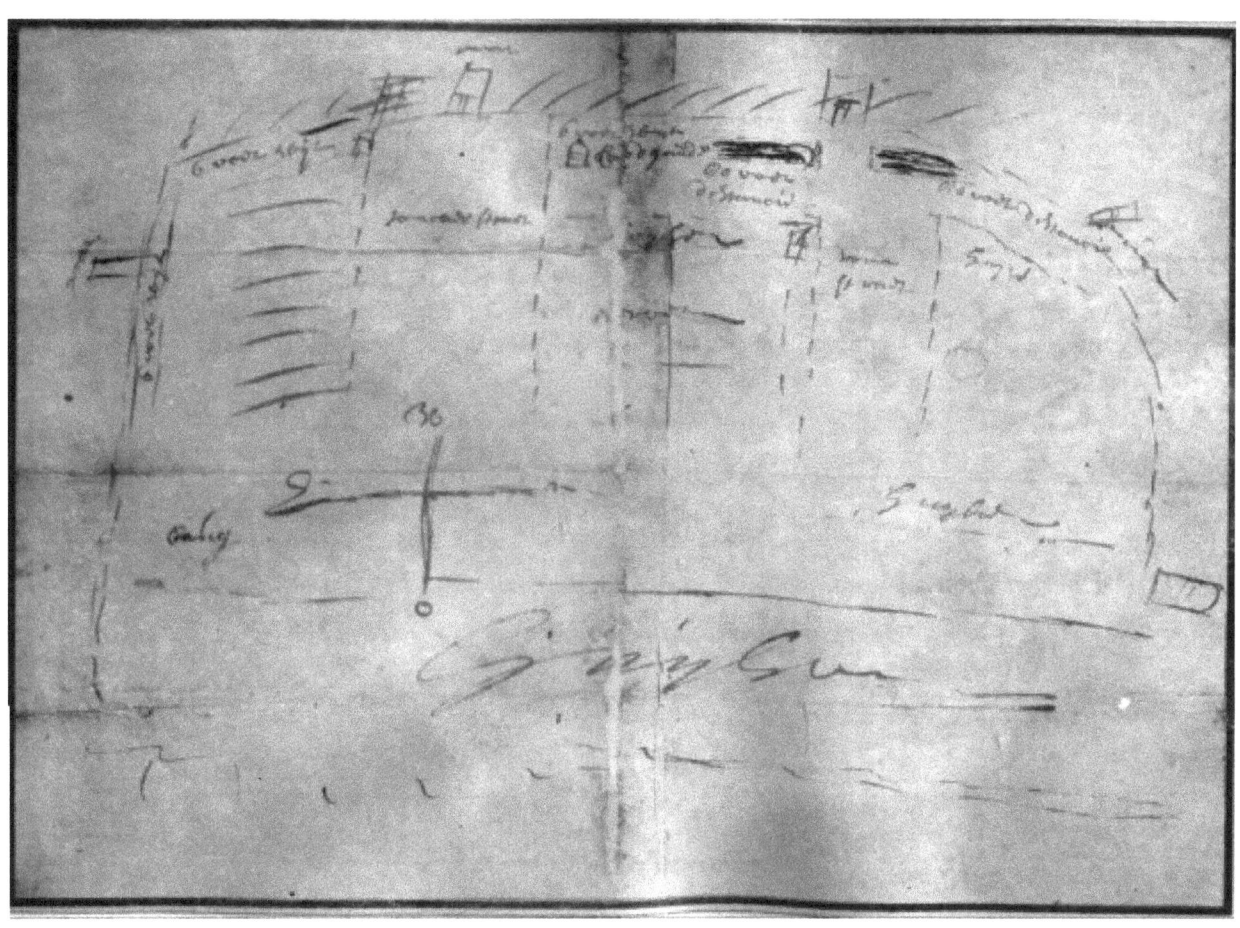

The oldest map of Albany showing the 1659 plank wall was identified by John Wolcott.

Let's look at a few of observations. No matter what Tantillo or any other artist paints of Fort Nassau neither have an idea what it looks like really. We all know the dimensions of the site, it's been published for 400 years, and the facts are the facts. What part of the facts don't you like? There are no elevations or profiles printed anywhere. The only thing we have of any real depiction or clue is a description by De Laet in 1625 and in an 18th century English edition of a French book of fortifications by Sebastian Vauban. It shows almost exactly the layout of Fort Nassau as described on the Block 1614 map, the only such depiction in the entire book-almost as a last thought addition as if the author just found it. He also calls it a redoubt not a fort and gives us some idea of the profile. There is no mention of the trading house inside. De Laet wrote in 1625 *"the fort was built in the form of a redoubt, surrounded by a moat eighteen feet wide, it was mounted with two pieces of cannon and eleven pederros [guns that shot stones]."*

John has pointed out that Tantillo's latest painting looks eerily like the Canadian trading post of Tadousac (1600) (See this photo at http://sixtyrising.files.wordpress.com/2013/07/poste-de-traite-chauvin0atrading-post-1600-1942-1111.jpg) described by Samuel Champlain in his voyages. This

Chauvin's trading post repro. From
http://www.ezcruising.net/page/4/

Compare Tantillo's Fort Nassau painting with this
http://www.lftantillo.com/shop/17th-Century/The-Trading-House/prod_63.html

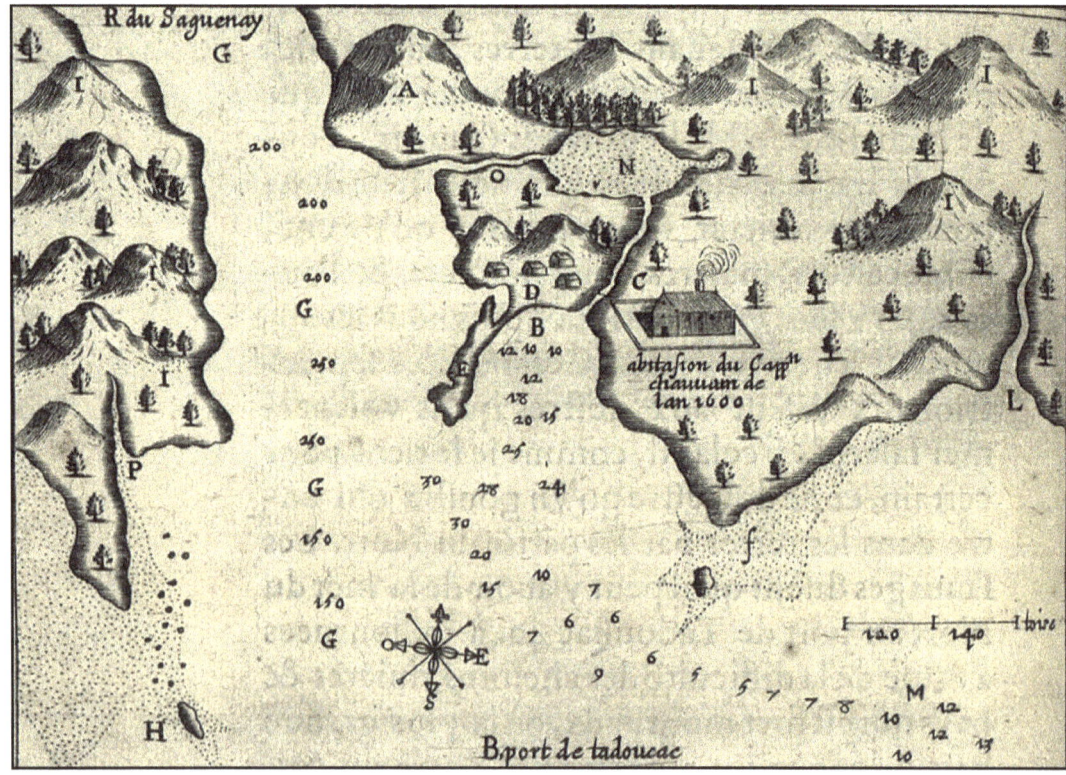

Champlain's map of Tadoussac showing Chauvin's house. From
https://darcynord.wordpress.com/tag/montagnais/

reproduction however does not look like Champlain's drawing, but may be based on the "replica" Chauvin's house that is located at present Tadousac which has been criticized as inaccurate and that was designed by William Coverdale, director of the Canada Steamship Company in 1943 to make money from unknowing tourists.

Wolcott points out that Tadousac was 25 feet long and 18 feet wide, covered with boards and encompassed by a wall made of wattle and had a ditch and no bastions. But did the French have it as planks rather than boards (probably thick planks) and besides Champlain's little drawing doesn't look exactly that way. Interestingly, 18 feet wide is the figure for Fort Nassau's moat and 25 feet for Tadousac is basically the same as the width as the 26-foot width of Fort Nassau. Tantillo has published his 3D rendition in the Times Union (see http://www.timesunion.com/local/article/Centuries-old-question-mdash-where-was-Fort-5767896.php). I do like his modeling but am perplexed by his locating two bastions at the fort when there is no description of that in the records. There are no archeological or historical records supporting this?

I also do not agree with his assertion that the first fort was in the middle of the island (I suggested that a second edition of the fort was in the middle). It would have been close to the mouth of the Normanskill and Island Creek; closer to the where the Indigenous people would be canoeing or hiking down from the Mohawk Valley to trade (Tantillo's first rendition shown in Dunn's book did have it here so apparently he changed his mind, three more times I might add since I have seen four different Tantillo depictions of Fort Nassau, hence the title of this article). Why create a longer travel distance if you don't have to do it? I also have a copy of a map that shows two projections out into Island Creek near there. Enticing.

If one took the time to do any research you would notice that most forts of the period are placed close to bodies of water for transportation, and close to fresh water streams for potable water, unless you can dig a well.

There are two observations that make me believe that Fort Nassau had horizontal walls and not very high ones at that. Of course the whole issue of vertical vs. horizontal is an academic one but would have been important from a security point. First, Fort Orange built on the mainland in 1624 had horizontal planks or logs. We know that from the archeological record. Additionally, the first map of Albany (Beverwyck) that Wolcott dates at 1659, thirty-five years after the building of Fort Orange, also has horizontal planks surrounding the settlement. As an additional piece of evidence so did the first fortification across Manhattan (Wall Street, 1653) around

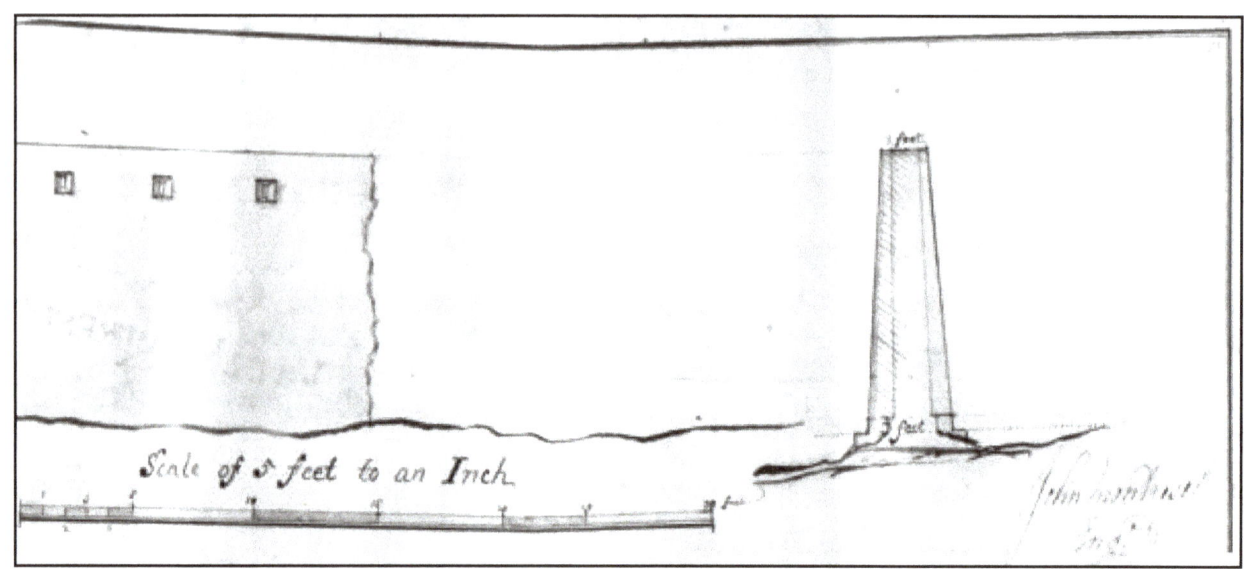

Albany's temporary stone wall of 1734. Source: DR.

the same time further south inferring this may have been the normal way to build a defensive wall at that time.

The first use of vertical stockade posts in Albany, as described in the literature, is the 1670 stockade wall since vertical posts were found in excavations. Albany even tried and began to build a stone wall around it in 1734 but the provincial government was too cheap to fund it so they took the one section they built down. They still had vertical posts in 1756.

Vertical stockade posts came into use in 1670 like these seen in this Albany excavation. Photo: DR

So my question is this. If the earliest known protective walls around Albany (Fort Orange in 1624, the village (Beverwyck) in 1659, and even Manhattan) were horizontal, isn't it logical to think that earlier Fort Nassau had horizontal walls? To think a different way means they used vertical walls in 1614-1617, then horizontal ones from

124

> **BOOK V.**
>
> **CHAP. I.**
>
> IN regard that Fortification is either Continual, or Transitory, we shall now speak of the latter, as having given full Instructions for the first: Let us begin with a Redoubt.
>
> *Of the Raising a Redoubt.*
>
> 1. Make a Rectangle Square, each side of which contains from 12 to 20 Fathoms.
> 2. Within this Square draw the Base of the Rampart three Fathoms large; and that of the Parapet from 9 to 10 Feet. The Height of the Rampart above the Level of the Feild ought to be three Feet; and that of the Parapet above the Plat-
>
> 90 *A Treatise of Fortification,* **Book V.**
>
> Platform of the Rampart, of five, as is usual: or of seven, when there are two Steps or Banquets: though sometimes they raise the Rampart a little higher, as necessity requires.
>
> 3. About the Rampart toward the Field draw another Parallel three Feet wide, which is call'd the *Berme*.
> 4. About the *Berme* make a Moat of four fathoms, with a Rounding before the Points of the exterior Sides: the Depth of the Moat ought to be about eight or ten Feet.
> 5. The Bridge for entrance into the Redoubt ought to be ten or twelve Feet broad, when you would bring the Cannon into it; otherwise five or six Feet of breadth will suffice. See the Plate Q. *Fig.* XXVIII. in *Chap.* 14. *Lib.* 4.

Vauban's explanation of the plan that is similar to Fort Nassau. Source: John Wolcott.

1624 to 1659, then went back to vertical walls after that? Why? Doesn't seem logical. It does not mean it could not have happen, but humans are pretty conservative animals. It seems unlikely that they would do it one way, change, and then go back to the other way?

Wolcott does not think the first defensive wall around Fort Nassau was very large, or tall, because they would have only been used to defend against arrows, not cannon or muskets. So it may have only been tall enough to stand behind. Vertical posts (10 feet tall) would have been needed later as the Dutch were competing with the French and English who had better weapons. That is not cast in stone but just seems a logical thought. According to Wolcott, Fort Nassau was built during the 12-year truce so they were not worried about attacks by the Spanish, and not too worried about the French or English.

Also the discussion about an earlier French Chateau or castle on the island before Fort Nassau is rubbish. There is no archeological or documentary evidence to prove it. In 1653 Adrian Van Der Donck dismissed the Spanish connection. Even Dankers and Sluyter later in 1679 reported that there was rumor that the Spanish built the fort there and dismissed it.

Tantillo stated that he doesn't think any remains of Fort Nassau exist. He states, *"It also wasn't ruggedly built and it's possible that whatever structure there was is completely gone. I think it's very doubtful that archaeologists will be able to find any remains of Fort Nassau, so the debate over the location isn't really that important to me."*

Well it is important to me since it is the beginning of Albany's history.

However Tantillo is just plain wrong. Forty-three years after the fort was flooded out, Peter Stuyvesant in writing to the General Court of Massachusetts in 1660 reported that the small fort which the Dutch built there *"an island near Fort Orange yet bears the name of Castle Island, and the monuments of which can yet be shown."* Even he thought it was destroyed but even with the continued deterioration of the fort, Dankers and Sluyter, nineteen (19) years after Stuyvesant writing, in 1679, after the fort was supposedly destroyed, described the remains of the fort:

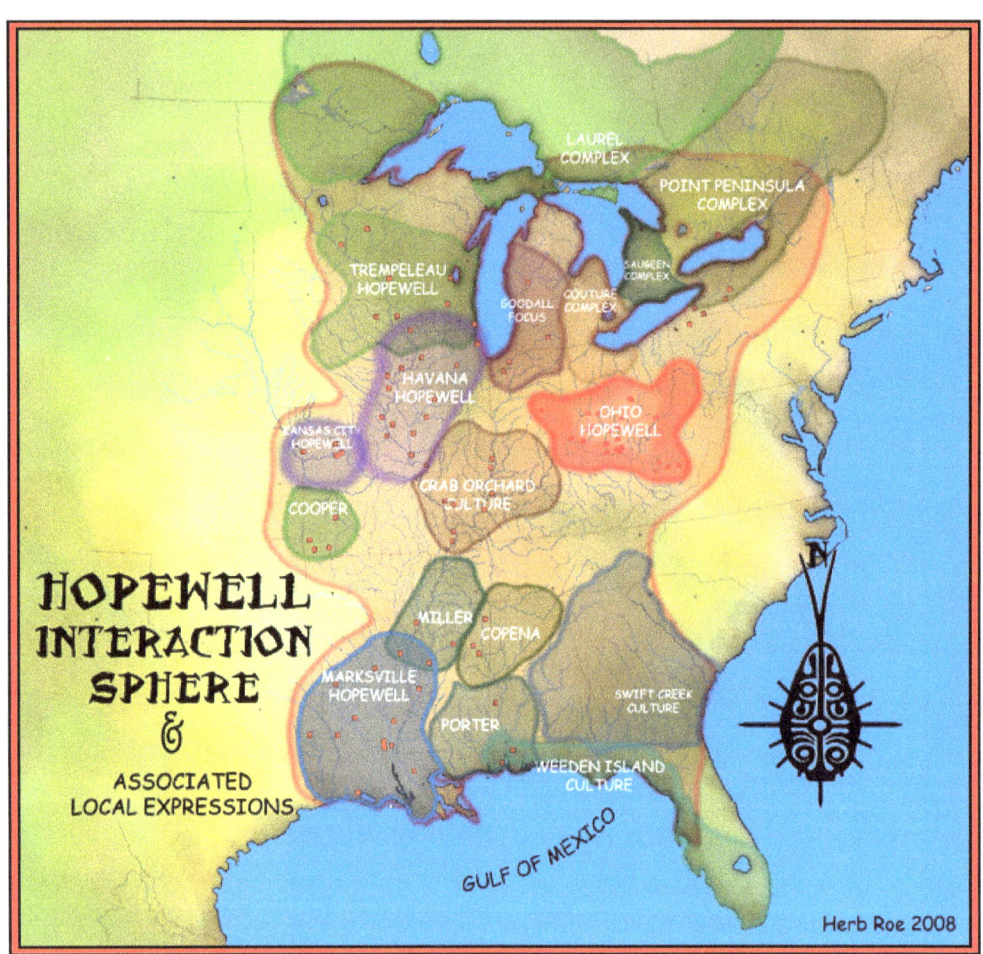

Mound Builders extension into NYS. Source: Wikipedia

*In the afternoon, we took a walk to an island upon the end of which there is a fort built, they say, by the Spaniards. That a fort has been there is evident enough from the earth thrown up and strewn around, but it is not to be supposed that the Spaniards came so far inland to build forts, when there are no monuments of them to be seen elsewhere and down on the sea coasts, where, however, they have been according to the traditions of the Indians. This spot is a short hour's distance below Albany, on the west side of the river.*

Well it seems to have survived sixty-five years of flooding them, so why wouldn't there be any evidence now? And how does he know it "wasn't ruggedly built." Where in the historical or archeological records does it say that? Prove it! In fact, it appears from the records that it was abandoned and any good archeologist knows that silting over the site will preserve it.

The whole idea that the French built and earlier Fort Nassau also makes the rounds — the chateau or "castle." Nicolas Wassenaer writing in 1624-5 but referring to 1614 wrote that the Dutch built a "kastell" on the island. Indian villages at the time were also called castles.

Monks Mound built c 950-1100 located at the Cohokia Mounds near Collinsville, Illinois. Largest prehistoric earthwork in the United States. From Wikipedia.

The most likely answer however is that the early Dutch had found the remains of earthworks (called Indian Mounds) on Castle Island. They have been found throughout New York State and in the Ohio Valley they were created by the "Mound Builders;" that's right, they were made by indigenous people. The mound builders during a 5000-year period built various styles and shapes of earthen mounds used for religious, ceremonial, burial and residential use. What is known as the Woodland and Mississippian period (3400 BC to 16th century CE) mound builders were present around the Great Lakes, Ohio River Valley, Mississippi River Valley and environs. The Mississippian complex (circa 900-1450 CE) spread throughout the eastern US along the river valleys. The Spanish exploring the Southeast in 1540-42 encountered many mound builders and wrote about it.

There are hundreds — well at one time there were hundreds — of earthworks located in New York State when the Europeans landed. Earthworks were reported in 17 New York State counties in 1851. I personally know where there is one in Rensselaer County that is 800 feet long, 200 feet wide and 33 feet high. There is another in Grandville that is flat topped. Indian Hill in Montgomery County is another and is also on the Hudson River. Here is a nice video on the subject at:

https://www.youtube.com/watch?v=Yg9ZXvulMQE

If any part of the statement is true, it is likely that the Dutch traders built Fort Nassau on top of an abandoned earthwork, or had permission by the local Mohicans to do so. There are records that even the natives did not know who built the mounds at the time. Since very little was known of Native American customs an abandoned Indigenous mound could have easily been mistaken for European origins, since they were Eurocentric and did not think indigenous peoples had technology.

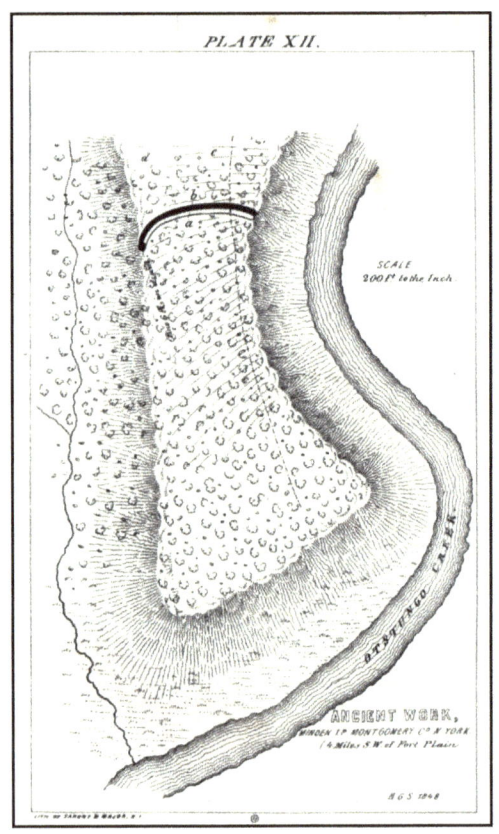

Native earthworks in Montgomery County. Could a similar earthwork been used to build Fort Nassau on in the Hudson River?

This story of a French fort was published in the 19th century with no citations to back it up. Most real historians don't even give it a second thought. There even is a fellow who wrote an article "debunking" the French Fort myth (see http://newyorkhistoryblog.org/2014/09/08/debunking-the-french-fort-on-albanys-castle-island/). Seems to be a lot of attempts of debunking going on lately.

Many of the "Indian mounds" have been obliterated by farming in NYS over the years. A 19th century NYS archeologist published details of their locations. We also know from documentation that the Native population built their own fortifications of various sizes. Champlain and Cartier observed that some Iroquois fortification had 20-foot high walls and one had a quadruple interlock palisade 30 feet high. Historically there were mounds found in Erie, Genesee, Monroe, Livingston, St. Lawrence, Oswego, Chenango, and Delaware counties. The famous Alligator Mound in Grandvile, Ohio measures 200 feet long and is five feet high.

So if there was an "abandoned fort" on Castle Island, Fort Nassau could have easily had been built on top of a Native earthwork. There should be plenty to find in the archeological record.

However, there is only way to find out the truth. DIG. We need to locate the locations.

John Wolcott and I are not trying to "debunk" anyone. We are seeking the truth. I have known John Wolcott for over 40 years and have never found him wrong when it comes to the history of Albany. I cannot say that about the others.

You see Wolcott and I can't lose. If it turns out we are wrong about our location of Fort Nassau on Castle Island and it is in a location other than the three I predict, or the one that John predicts, we still don't lose. Our efforts are purely to locate the remains of the fort for historical and heritage tourism purposes, not as an ego trip. If this race to be right to find its location is successful, we still have accomplished our goals.

Often when you try to save ecosystems you have to deal with egosystems. Tantillo should be more interested in trying to find the truth rather than trying to debunk Wolcott who clearly is superior in research skills. Wolcott's response to all this is that Tantillo's criticism to his location is representative on his part a rather temperamental bit of pique and seeming desperation. He is very disappointed that he didn't even extend the common courtesy and objectivity of having reviewed John's evidence. As for the quality of his evidence, which he seems to have ignored, John can only say, *"res ipsa loquitir."*

We didn't light the fire.

WPA Report (21 pages) on projects in the Capital District published in 1936.

# We Need a 2020 "New Deal" Public Works Program
First published on May 4, 2020 at 3:21 am

Twenty-million Americans filed for unemployment already with more to come. Most sources are comparing this to the great Depression of the 20s and 30's. During that time President Franklin Roosevelt created his New Deal Program that comprised a number of works projects to get people working again. Notable were the Federal Emergency Relief Administration (FERA, 1933, formerly the Emergency Relief Administration (ERA)); the Work Projects Administration (WPA, 1935), which replaced FERA in 1935; the Civilian Conservation Corp (CCC, 1933); and the Historic American Buildings Survey (HABS, 1933). Others included the Farm Security Administration (FSA), the National Industrial Recovery Act of 1933 (NIRA) and the Social Security Administration (SSA).

There are now a number of elected officials talking about creating a new version of the WPA. I believe a new version of WPA, CCC and HABS should also be considered.

### The Works Progress Administration (WPA)
The Works Progress Administration (WPA; renamed in 1939 as the Work Projects Administration) was part of Roosevelt's American New Deal agency that employed millions of mostly unskilled men to carry out public works projects. This included construction of public buildings and roads, laying sidewalks, creating parks, a Federal Writer's Project, and more.

According to the Library of Congress, At its peak in 1938, the *"WPA provided paid jobs for three million unemployed men and women, as well as youth in a separate division, the National Youth Administration. Between 1935 and 1943, when the agency was disbanded, the WPA employed 8.5 million people. Most people who needed a job were eligible for employment in some capacity. Hourly wages were typically set to the prevailing wages in each area. Full employment, which was reached in 1942 and emerged as a long-term national goal around 1944, was not the goal of the WPA; rather, it tried to provide one paid job for all families in which the breadwinner suffered long-term unemployment."*

The LOC also reported that in one project, Federal Project Number One, the WPA employed musicians, artists, writers, actors and directors in large arts, drama, media, and literacy projects. The five projects dedicated to these were: the Federal Writers' Project (FWP), the Historical Records Survey (HRS), the Federal Theatre Project (FTP), the Federal Music Project (FMP), and the Federal Art Project (FAP).

In the Historical Records Survey, for instance, many former slaves in the South were interviewed. Theater and music groups toured throughout the United States, and gave more than 225,000 performances. Archaeological investigations under the WPA were influential in the rediscovery of prehistoric Native American cultures, and the development of professional archaeology in the US.

The WPA was a national program that operated its own projects in cooperation with state and local governments, which provided 10–30% of the costs. It ended on June 30, 1943, as a result of low unemployment due to the worker shortage of World War II. The WPA had provided millions of Americans with jobs for eight years.

**Civilian Conservation Corps (CCC)**

The Civilian Conservation Corps (CCC) was a voluntary public work relief program that operated from 1933 to 1942 basically for unemployed and single men. Originally it was designed for ages 18–25 but it later expanded to ages 17–28. The CCC was a major part of Roosevelt's New Deal that provided manual labor jobs related to the conservation and development of natural resources in rural lands owned by federal, state, and local governments. The program was designed to provide jobs and to relieve the stress that millions of families who had problems finding jobs during the Depression

At one time there was 300,000 men working and over nine years three million participated in the program. By working on a CCC project the person received shelter, clothing, food, and $30 a month (now worth $590 in 2019). The young worker had to send home $25 of that to his family. Not only did the CCC become the most popular of the New Deal, it provided a healthy environment, improved their physical strength and increased their chances of getting a job. It also increased appreciation for nature and natural resources. It was a time when early environmentalists like Aldo Leopold was writing and helping develop an environmental philosophy towards stewardship. In 1935 Leopold and Arthur Carhardt created the Wilderness Society. A year later The National Wildlife Society was formed.

Remember the great Dust Bowl of the Great Plains also occurred at this time in 1933. Throughout its history some 2,000 CCC camps were open, millions of trees were planted, and roads, fire towers, buildings and bridges and many other public works are built. More than 2.5 million people served until the program ended in 1942 due to World War II and the draft. Other federal programs, including the Tennessee Valley Authority and the Soil Conservation Service, also started during FDR presidency.

The CCC operated separate programs for veterans and Native Americans. Approximately 15,000 Native Americans participated in the program, helping them deal with the Depression.

Much of the CCC operated in the Adirondacks but covered the whole State. They planted trees for example, some six million in 1934 in one location. There were 20 CCC Camps throughout the State in 1933. Camp number 72 was located in Delmar and the work related to fish and game work on a grouse farm (Now Delmar's Five Rivers). Two camps, numbers 77 and 78, were in Cherry Plain in Rensselaer County. Camp 77 worked on truck trails and cut line between refuge and hunting grounds. Camp 78 worked on fish and game work, cleaning areas for flooding. The camp had 400 men on the Capital District Game Refuge and worked on stream development of the Black River and included stocking with fingerling brook trout. The Delmar Game Farm was established during this time with a goal to develop better and more economical ways of artificially propagating game birds and animals. Special attention was given to Ruffed Grouse but also quail and pheasants. It is now known as Five Rivers Environmental Education Center. Cherry Plain State Park was the other result.

**The Historic American Buildings Survey (HABS)**

In 1933, The Historic American Buildings Survey (HABS) became America's first federal preservation program to document America's architectural heritage. The government was noticing the destruction of much of our history in the name of progress. Creation of the program was motivated primarily by this perceived need to *"mitigate the negative effects upon our history and culture of rapidly vanishing architectural resources."* This was also happening at the same time that historic Williamsburg was being restored and the historic and national sites were being developed within the National Park System.

According to the Library of Congress, *"Architects interested in the colonial era had previously produced drawings and photographs of historic architecture, but only on a limited, local, or regional basis. A source was needed to assist with the documentation of our architectural heritage, as well as with design and interpretation of historic resources, that was national in scope. As it was stated in the tripartite agreement between the American Institute of Architects, the Library of Congress, and the NPS that formed HABS, "A comprehensive and continuous national survey is the logical concern of the Federal Government." As a national survey, the HABS collection is intended to represent "a complete resume of the builder's art." Thus, the building selection ranges in type and style from the monumental and architect-designed to the utilitarian and vernacular, including a sampling of our nation's vast array of regionally and ethnically derived building traditions."*

Thousands of photographs and detailed drawings were produced many from the Capital District. It did not stop the destruction of the historic sites however and in many cases, especially in the Capital District, the photographs and drawings of important historic sites are all that exist.

## LOCAL WPA PROJECTS

During the WPA era there were several notable WPA projects in the Capital District.

## ALBANY

**The Federal Post Office (Now James T. Foley US Court House) on Broadway.**

The James T. Foley US Court House on Broadway was built in 1934-34. This was actually built as the Post Office. The building had an exterior bridge connecting the nearby rail station with the post office and occupied the entire first two floors. Inside this beautiful building was a series of murals painted by Ethel Parsons: *"Marble pilasters divide the main lobby into nine bays, each articulated with a ceiling mural. Artist Ethel M. Parsons painted the oil-on-canvas murals in 1935, depicting each of the seven continents as well as the North Pole and the United States. Interspersed with the murals are plaster plaques by Italian artist Enea*

The Federal Post Office on Broadway was built in 1935. WPA Photo from 1935.

*Biafora Portraying famous Americans, including Abraham Lincoln, Benjamin Franklin, and George Washington, as portrayed on the earliest US postage stamps. With the exception of the murals, the ceiling is covered with aluminum leaf."*

One of Parson's beautiful murals in the former post office.

Parsons who was a painter, engraver, and textile designer has a number of works that can be found in St. Bartholomew's Church, Church of St. Vincent Ferrer, NY; St. Stephen's Church, Stevens Point, WI; Mutual Casualty Ins. Bldg.; Stevens Point, WI; Christ Church, West Haven, CT; Trinity Church, Ft. Wayne, IN; Church of the Epiphany, Roslyn, LI, NY; Brooke General Hospital Chapel, US Army, San Antonio, TX; stained glass windows: Dana Chapel, Madison Ave. Presbyterian Church, N.Y; St. John's Episcopal Church, Bernardsville, NJ, 1961; portrait, ex-pres., John Henry Barrows, Oberlin College, and 1958; 30 religious triptychs for US Armed Forces. 1962-64.

In the post office/court house, she painted large maps each 15′ square, also decorations for ceilings in two court rooms, three judge's rooms, postmaster's room, seven lobbies, stair halls and elevator lobbies. There is a great bio of Ethel by her great niece on the Web showing great photos of her work in the post office building. You can read it here: https://gplart.com/ethel-parsons-paullin

Photo of Parsons. Source her great niece's website that has an excellent bio on Ethel. https://gplart.com/ethel-parsons-paullin

## Loudonville Reservoir

Located in Colonie off Albany-Shaker Road the Loudonville Reservoir's Basin C was constructed by the WPA. In a 1940 report it stated:

*"Basin C, Loudonville Reservoir, huge concrete retainer, holds 93,000,000 gallons, a guarantee of ten days supply for Albany against any stoppage. Worked with double shifts excavation exceeded rate set on Basins A and B, build under private contract. Concrete was laid in 98 days. ... The City of Albany several years ago expended more than $6,000,000 to develop a mountain water supply eliminating the old supply that was derived from the Hudson River. The new WPA built Basin was the last link in the new supply."*

Here is a video showing the construction: https://www.criticalpast.com/video/65675064809_Works-Progress-Administration_water-reservoir_workers-constructing_women-stitch-garments

## Bleecker Stadium
**Bleecker Stadium, Clinton Ave. between Swinburne Park and Ontario St.**

This could be considered one of the early adapted-reuse projects. Bleecker Stadium is one of the largest man made earthen structures in the world. Originally part of a

Building the reservoir in May and October 1936. WPA Photo.

The reservoir today. From the All Over Albany Web site, 2015.

complex of conduits and reservoirs it supplied Albanians with drinking water from the Pine Bush during the 19th century. In 1934 it was turned into a stadium *"It seats 10,000 and has two baseball fields, a football field, a quarter-mile track, jumping and vaulting pits, and tennis courts."* Originally started by Roosevelt's Temporary Emergency Relief Administration (TERA) program it was finished by the WPA in 1940 when they built the Georgian colonial style clubhouse.

Bleecker today. Photo from the Stadium Website.

Building Bleecker Stadium in 1934. WPA photo. Albany Institute of History and Art photo.

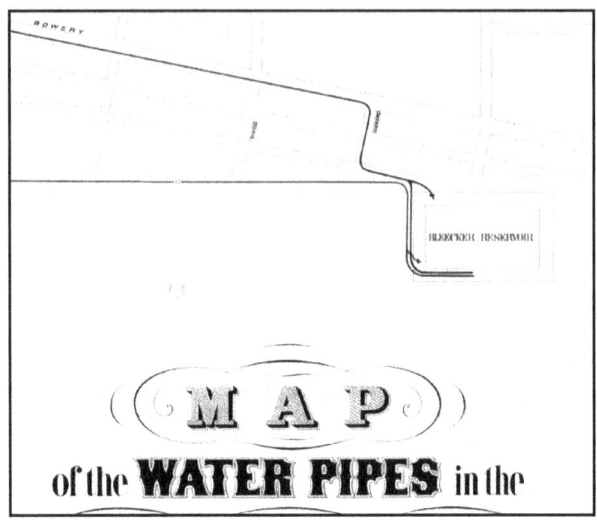 

Bleecker Reservoir in 1860 showing location of distribution pipes.

Bleecker Stadium showing ball field and club house in back, circa 1940. Albany Institute of History and Art photo.

## Albany Guide

The WPA, through the Federal Writers' Project of New York State (American Guide Series) also published an "Albany Guide," a tour guide to the city. They also wrote "New York – A Guide to the Empire State" in 1940. You can read it here: https://hdl.handle.net/2027/mdp.39015019212193

Other Albany projects included paved mile of city streets with red and yellow brick (some can be seen on West Lawrence and Kent Streets)

## TROY

Troy also had WPA projects. The current post office on Fourth Street was begun in 1936 and finished in 1938, replacing the previous post office on the same site. There are two murals in the lobby painted by artist Waldo Peirce in 1939. He was known as "the American Renoir." See his biography at https://en.wikipedia.org/wiki/Waldo_Peirce

The two murals are entitled "Rip Van Winkle" and "Legends of the Hudson."

Waldo Peirce and his Legends of the Hudson mural in the Troy post office lobby.

## Troy Reservoir
**Unknown location in Troy.**

The WPA constructed a reservoir for the City of Troy in 1937. I haven't been able to locate the exact location but there is a photograph of it.

Where's Waldo? Found him on Wikipedia. Photo from the 1930s.

## Spring Avenue Parkland

Most people in Troy probably do not realize that the 2000 feet strip of land on Spring Avenue between Locust Avenue and Linden Avenue is a park and the road is called the Barker Parkway. There was a rallying cry there to develop a park along the road when Mayor James W. Fleming ran against Alderman John A. R. Kapp in 1921. Fleming vowed to:

*"Mayor Fleming Pledges the Immediate Development of Frear Park, the Barker Parkway and All Other Recreation Centers."*

WPA built reservoir in Troy. Unknown location. WPA Photo.

In 1928, Troy's Alderman Nielsen introduced a resolution requesting the city to provide shelters and benches on the Barker Parkway, on Spring Avenue. The resolution recited the fact that the city has men at work beautifying the park and gives commendation to the authorities for enhancing the value of land that was deeded to the city by Mrs. Stephen E. Barker and C. W. T. Barker. This resolution was adopted.

On May 19, 1933, the Troy Times announced the following:

*"Beautifying Barker Parkway.*
*The planting along the Barker Parkway on Spring Avenue of 2,800 pine trees turned over to the city by the Nature Study and Garden Division of the Troy Woman's Club calls attention to the possibilities of beautifying and making available to the public this fine gift of almost primitive woodland ravine in the very heart of industrial and business Troy. The earliest possible opportunity should be taken to plant there a variety of native trees to supplement the many stately elms and others and to replace the ancient deadwood which was removed after the property was presented to the city. Much work of this kind, with necessary grading and improving, can now be done as an unemployment project, looking forward to the time when the city's resources will permit of planting*

Barker Parkway, AKA Spring Avenue is supposed to be a dedicated park. However there seems to be a number of houses that were built after it was given to the city and should be investigated to see if it violated the donation by the Barker family.

Barker Parkway between Linden Ave (top left) and Locust Avenue (top right).

*shrubs, vines and flowers and laying out walks and adding a brook or two. Without any very extravagant outlay the Barker Parkway could be converted into one of the most beautiful and most accessible of city parks, an enticing resting place that would contribute to the delight of Trojans who love nature and enhance the beauty of one of the leading highways through the canter of the city."*

On January 17, 1934, it was announced that work was started that day for the beautification of Barker Parkway and *"Approximately 40 workers were engaged at first in grading and filling in the land and later three residences on the property will be removed and the property landscaped and improved."*

*"The land was acquired by the late Mrs. Stephen Barker and deeded to the city in 1919 for the purpose of a public park, which should preserve the rustic beauty of the drive. It is approximately 300 feet in width and extends a distance of approximately 2,000 feet from Locust Avenue toward Linden Avenue."*

On March 3, 1934, the city approved the park along Spring Avenue and for demolishing of the old buildings on the Barker Parkway (two wooden structures, one brick building).

In 1935 the commissioner of Public works recommended improvement of *"Barker Parkway on Spring Avenue by removal of billboards and other unsightly material and the conversion of the parkway into a picnic grounds as a pleasing entrance to the city proper and planting of trees on the slopes of Prospect Park, on Barker Parkway and along Campbell Avenue. "Parking facilities will be arranged and the parkway will be suitable for picnics." "Five thousand small pine trees received from the State Conservation Department are to be planted there."*

By the 1950s things look different. In the spring of 1954, the Troy Record put the city on notice:

## IT NEEDS CLEANING

*Entries into Troy should be as attractive as they can be made. First impressions are likely to influence permanent impressions. A dirty street into town implies carelessness on the part of the authorities and slipshod government.*

*One of the entries to Troy is Spring Avenue. It is a little more than an entry; it is a busy thoroughfare from a part of the Fifth Ward and beyond to the business center of the city. It should be attractive. It was given to Troy by the Barker family as a memorial. It is a beautiful wooded highway. It ought to be called Barker Parkway—and kept like a parkway. Or it ought to return to the picturesque name it possessed for a century—the Hollow Road.*

*At the present time it is unsightly. Debris lies along the curbs. Indeed, there is a certain amount of fire danger if a cigarette stub were dropped among the leaves and old papers that are lying about We do not blame the Public Works Department for this situation. At the end of the winter season there is more clean-up work to be done than any ordinary force can achieve promptly. It takes time to get things in shape. But we do hope Spring Avenue will be "redd" up very soon, it is one of the charming highways of the area and should be kept charming."*

Apparently things did not go so well and the area became neglected. An editorial in the Troy Record on May 2, 1961, said this:

"*Troy is sadly deficient in beauty. Our parks have few flowers and most of our shade trees have disappeared from the streets. Weed infested vacant lots are tolerated to an extent that assures the city the highest pollen count in the state. The city budget contains thousands of dollars appropriated to remove dead trees but not one dollar for shrubs or flowers. The main arteries of the city are neglected and weed grown to the point that traffic signs are obscured.*

*The Junior Chamber is demonstrating how a display of pride in the appearance of the community can work wonders. How splendid it would be for Troy to have other organizations follow suit. Spring Avenue, for instance, possesses great natural beauty. The thoroughfare should rightfully be known by its correct name—Barker Parkway. But how can a weed cluttered, vine tangled jungle along a main approach be termed a parkway? This travel artery, and others in Troy, could be transformed from ugliness to beauty by the city's civic and service bodies. In the event the members of the organizations stake out a piece of the city and accept responsibility for its improvement many helping hands will volunteer to assist And Commissioner Quigley will be first in line, we may be sure."*

That didn't do the trick so another editorial in August 2, 1961, said this:

*"An outstanding example of neglect of a potential beauty spot is found in Spring Avenue below Campbell Avenue, once known as the Old Hollow Road and more recently, Barker Parkway. The land adjoining the thoroughfare was given the city for park purposes. Instead, the strip along the thoroughfare is a jungle of weeds and vines. No great expense or effort would be required to transform the area into a place of beauty.*

*Barker Parkway will remain a tangle of weeds and underbrush as long as Trojans tolerate the neglect. Here is an opportunity for civic-minded Trojans to band together and make the site attractive. The beginning must be made at the citizen level. City planners and private citizens concerned for the morale of their home town on inquiring into the method used by other cities to relieve drabness by planting and decorating have discovered that citizen groups organize, plan and supervise the work. Trojans can work wonders in their city, if they care to do so."*

At one point in time a baseball diamond was put in the park for little league. In the 60's one of the springs that emanate from the glacial deposits was made into a public springs and thousands of people still use it today. There were many springs throughout the city in the 19th century where the Rensselaer Plateau ends at the river plain. There was one on 9th Street, North Fourth at the brewery of T. J. Sands (1870), one at "Mr. Lutzelberger's Park," and Sheldon & Green's foundry on Sixth Street, below Broadway and extending back to Seventh Street.

Other Troy projects included the Menands Bridge, renovations of public schools, sidewalks in Lansingburgh, removal of trolley tracks on Second Avenue, improvements of the Tomhannock and Quackenkill reservoirs and a new roof on City Hall.

## First Precinct Station House, South Troy

The First Precinct building was built just to the south of the firehouse on city owned property. It was occupied as a police station from 1900 to 1944 when all the precinct houses were consolidated in the Central Police Station located at the Northwest corner of State Street and 6th Avenue. While the Central Station was built in 1923 the precinct houses stayed intact until the 1940s.

In 1935-36, the building underwent repairs and a face lift as a WPA project. There is a plague on the front facade that says: "Improved by Works Progress Administration 1935-1936." A new facade was added as well as interior

A new entrance was added by the WPA in 1935-36 but the South facing building wall was not changed due to its hidden character by residences next to it. Photo by Don Rittner.

renovations. New brick work was added to the North facing wall but not the South facing wall. Throughout its history many arrests were carried out and the jails used. A corner of the building on the North facing wall on the East end was later filled in. This "Corner notch" was due to the fitting in of the building footprint abutting the fire tower that use to be located there. Shortly after the consolidation of the precincts into the central police station, the building became the American Legion and VFW Post Hall. The building at the time was listed as 318 Third Street. In 1952 it was VFW Post 628 and remained so until after the 1970s when it became a private residence or apartment house.

## Troy Armory

The original Troy Armory was located at the Southeast corner of Ferry and River Streets but burned in 1917. It was replaced in 1920 by the current building now own by RPI. In 1940 it received a $21,510 dollar WPA funding for *"improvement of the building and grounds of the Troy Armory… It was in line with national defense policy."*

In 1970, Rensselaer was finally able to finalize an agreement with New York State to purchase the Armory and nine acres of land between 15th St. and Burdett Ave. As part of the agreement, RPI would contribute $1.6 million and 20 acres of land in East Greenbush for a new Armory. It has been used for concerts and other events by the college since then.

Troy Armory. Photo by Don Rittner

## SCHENECTADY

In Schenectady, you will notice in some of the neighborhoods sidewalks with WPA stamped right in them. Most WPA projects focused on improving Schenectady's infrastructure. Fortunately we know a great deal about Schenectady WPA projects from student Scott F. Power who wrote a thesis at Union College in 2011 called *Schenectady's New Deal: An Investigation of the WPA in the City of Schenectady*.

Most of the following information is taken from his excellent thesis (no doubt getting an A). In his thesis he states that WPA workers built schools, highways, and parks. They constructed pressure outlets and dams, and built swimming pools and outdoor ice-skating rinks, built schools, highways, and parks. They installed 1.5 inch curbing along both sides of Lafayette Street, specifically between Hamilton Street and Union Street. In 1935 WPA workers graded and surfaced, with run of bank gravel, Fourteenth Street, Fifteenth Street, and Sixteen Street; all located within the city's Tenth Ward (Bellevue). To improve traffic conditions, they filled and widened the intersection at Duane Street and Altamont Avenue, thereby alleviating congestion. The majority of WPA projects in Schenectady between 1935 and 1941 included street repair and building construction, building renovation, and recreational improvements. In 1936, the WPA extended Watt Street between Altamont Avenue and Michigan Avenue in the Schenectady's Eighth Ward. The Central Fire Station on Erie Boulevard and Fire Station No. 7 located on Fourth Avenue were renovated, repaired, cleaned, and painted by relief workers who subsequently installed proper electrical work throughout both buildings. In July 1936, the Council appropriated $7,500.00 for the construction of several sewer outlets near Fuller Pond. Workers deepened and cleaned the creek situated at the Pleasant Valley Park and Fuller Pond draining outlet (currently situated between Park Road and Interstate 890 in the neighborhood of Hamilton Hills). The project also called for the Fuller Pond outlet sewer pipe, as well as the sewer pipes located on Van Guysling Avenue and Broadway. Similar improvement work was done on Ocean Street between Campbell Avenue and the city line. The construction included the building of catch basins, culverts, as well as the laying of sewer drains and gravel.

In January 1937, the Common Council appropriated $500.00 to repair the top floor of the Old Central Fire Station. Workers were asked to repaint, plaster, and rewire the fire station, as well as install necessary plumbing. Similarly, sanitary sewers and appurtenances were to be constructed on streets throughout the Fourteenth Ward (in the vicinity of Jay Street). Also in 1937, Elliot Street to State Street was graded, curbed, and surfaced with run of bank gravel, along with Marshall Avenue from State Street and Wagner Avenue between Albany Street and Watt Street. Similar work was done on Weaver Street in the vicinity of the railroad underpass. Sewers and catch basins were added to the street to facilitate adequate drainage along the lower elevation points of Weaver under the railroad. Concrete curbs and sidewalks were constructed along Ferry Street between State Street and Union Street to allow for adequate pedestrian traffic. Fire hydrants, catch basins, and telephone poles were installed along Ferry Street. Proper fill and grading facilitated the extension of Cheltingham Avenue to Osterlitz Avenue near the intersection of Osterlitz and Poplar. Poplar Street was then graded between Broad Street and Osterlitz, followed by the installation of a one hundred and fifty foot reinforced concrete culvert, bituminous macadam, and storm sewers to facilitate the flow of rain and river water. In 1938 a 6 inch water main was installed under Eastholm Road between State Street and Consaul Road, followed by the necessary curbing, paving, and grading required for its proper installation. The WPA demolished the Second Police Precinct located on Third Avenue and erected a new building complete with plumbing, heating, and electrical work. The WPA also built or refurbished park and recreational facilities throughout Schenectady. Five outdoor ice skating rinks were constructed throughout the city in 1936. Located in Central Park, Hillhurst Park, Riverside Park, Second Ward Park, and Willet Street playground, these ice skating rinks provided an outdoor recreation option for local residents and families. In 1936, the pool located in Riverside Park was renovated. Workers installed showers, constructed a springboard, and built a bathhouse complete with restrooms and changing facilities. In 1937, the playground at Howe School was reconstructed. WPA workers installed new equipment, steps, fencings, and proper drainage to allow for youth recreational activity within the Baker Avenue neighborhood. In addition, the WPA created hot beds and potting houses in Central Park and Pleasant Valley Park, therefore contributing to the beautification of Schenectady's parks and recreational facilities. In April 1938, workers helped coordinate leisure activities that included the establishment of several athletic leagues, specifically, a basketball, hockey, and soccer league, as well as boxing, wrestling, and handball association. Thus, the WPA contributed to the development of local recreation. Out of the forty-eight projects created, eight of them were not blue-collar construction in nature.

A few of the major WPA projects include:

**The Steinmetz Park Pool**

Originally called the Second Ward Park, in 1935 *"WPA workers constructed a wall of fieldstone around the pond,"* turning it into what was for years a popular swimming pool. The pond still exists but is no longer used for swimming."

The Steinmetz Park Pool

**Schenectady Municipal Golf Course**

This WPA project started in 1933 and was designed by golfer A. F. Knight, the inventor of the famous "Schenectady Putter," and *Jim Thompson. See my 2009 article on Knight here:*
https://web.archive.org/web/20200525143559/http://blog.timesunion.com:80/rittner/puttering-into-fame/299/

The club house is sitting atop a 10,000 year old sand dune from the former Albany Pine Barrens that once covered Schenectady. Photo from their Web site.

*The golf course was finished in 1935 and was funded by the precursor to the WPA; the Federal Emergency Relief Administration (FERA, begun in 1933 and the Civil* Works Administration (CWA, 1933-34)) workers (and possibly WPA workers) constructed this golf course. *"The Course stretches to 6600 yards (6000 m) and features fast, undulating greens and tight fairways blanketed within grasses and native vegetation. It was ranked by Golf Digest "Best Places to Play in 2004" and earned a three-star rating." Those undulating greens are sand dunes from the former Pine Barrens that covered most of Schenectady. It has the highest sand dune in elevation in the former Albany Pine Barrens. Over 1400 people worked on this project.*

### Schenectady Post Office Extension

This project started in 1933 and took two years to complete. The historic main post office was originally constructed in 1912 and received a New Deal extension undertaken on the East side between 1933 and 1935.

### Gifford Road Improvement

This WPA project worked to improve Gifford Road in Schenectady in 1939. WPA work included *"grading, surfacing, installing drainage facilities, digging ditch, changing course of creek,"* and performing related tasks. Of the $7,555 total cost of the project, the WPA appropriated $5,255.

Schenectady Post Office Extension.

### Post Office Mural In Scotia

Inside the post office is a WPA sponsored mural titled "The Glen Family Spared by French and Indians—1690." Sponsored the New Deal Treasury Section of Fine Arts. It was painted by artist Amy Jones (1899–1992) in 1941. It is 5'6" by 12' depicting the sparing of the Glen family during the 1690 Schenectady massacre, a key turning point in the early history of Scotia.

Her bio states this: *"Amy Jones was an American artist and muralist and was one of the founding members of the Saranac Lake Art League. Though most known for her watercolors, like Sandy Acre that is in the permanent collection of the Smithsonian American Art Museum, Jones also did illustration work for magazines and books. She won national competitions to*

From the "The Living New Deal" web site: https://livingnewdeal.org/projects/post-office-mural-scotia-ny/ Title: "The Glen Family Spared by French and Indians–1690" Painted by Amy Jones in 1941.

*complete post office murals for the post offices in Winsted, Connecticut; Painted Post, New York and Scotia, New York. Several major US corporations hold over twenty of her works.*

## HISTORIC AMERICAN BUILDINGS SURVEY (HABS)

The Historic American Buildings Survey (HABS) and the Historic American Engineering Record (HAER) was another New Deal program. This program was designed to document achievements in architecture, engineering, and landscape design in the United States and its territories through a comprehensive range of building types, engineering technologies, and landscapes. The Library of Congress holds the photos and documentation.

Amy Jones. From Wikipedia.

*"Administered since 1933 through cooperative agreements with the National Park Service, the Library of Congress, and the private sector, ongoing programs of the National Park Service have recorded America's built environment in multiformat surveys comprising more*

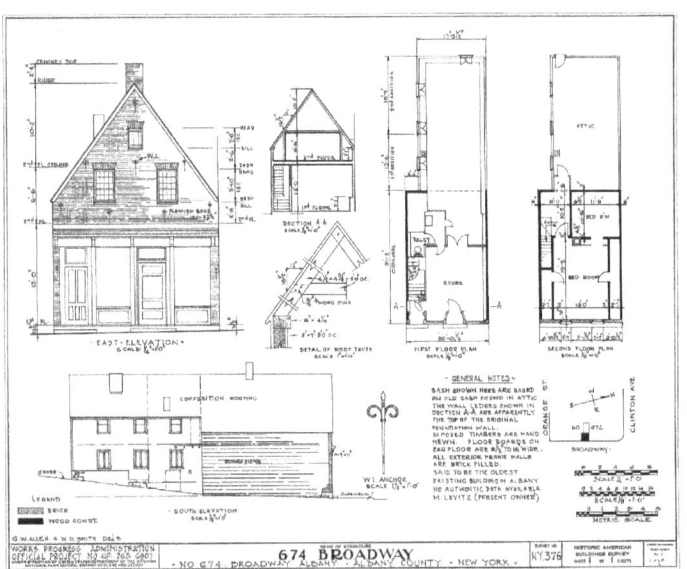

Above and below. Albany Dutch House on 674 Broadway in Albany. Photo and drawings from HABS program around 1933. From HABS, Library of Congress. Example of WAP historic survey. Building is demolished.

674 Broadway Dutch House. LOC Photo.

*than 581,000 measured drawings, large-format photographs, and written histories for more than 43,000 historic structures and sites dating from Pre-Columbian times to the twentieth century."*

The Historic American Buildings Survey (HABS) began during the Great Depression in December 1933, when Charles E. Peterson of the National Park Service submitted a proposal for one thousand out-of-work architects to spend ten weeks documenting *"America's antique buildings."*

HABS became a permanent program of the National Park Service in July 1934 and was formally authorized by Congress as part of the Historic Sites Act of 1935. The Historic American Engineering Record (HAER) was founded in 1969 to parallel HABS, providing for documentation of engineering works and industrial sites. In October 2000, the Historic American Landscapes Survey (HALS) was permanently established to document historic landscapes. The HABS/HAER/HALS collections are at the Library of Congress. Today's documentation is produced primarily by students pursuing degrees in architecture and in history, and the HABS, HAER and HALS programs have proven to be an important training ground for several generations of architects, engineers and historians.

## "NEW" NEW DEAL CAPITAL DISTRICT PROJECTS

So what could we do with a New New Deal in the Capital District?

In Troy, photograph every building, do a historic inventory of the remaining historic structures and compile a searchable database and add individual histories that anyone can explore.

Turn Barker Parkway into the park it was dedicated to be in the 1930s. There is ample room to put picnic benches, plants some trees (again) and flowerbeds. Perhaps some walking trails off the road. Fix up the spring works.

Rescue Prospect Park. Bring it back to its early twentieth century splendor. FIX the damn swimming pool. There are only four like in the world.

Bring back Mt. Ida Preserve. People have been using the falls for enjoyment for centuries. There will always be a few nuts that will kill themselves jumping off the cliff. You don't prevent everyone from enjoying it because of a handful. Never understood that logic. Stop being ashamed that you're the home of Uncle Sam. Embrace it. Create a museum if you must but stop ignoring the fact that it's America's

Icon and the city is connected with it. No more Brother Jonathan. Create a Bell Museum. There is thousands of Troy made bells ringing around the world. Promote it. Open up the riverfront. Turn what's left of the Burden Horseshoe Buildings in South Troy into a Quincy Market. Get rail back to Troy. The original Troy & Greenbush Railroad still goes to Adams Street, where there once was a train station. Guess what that rail is rated suitable for passenger service. Take down the Taylor Apartments, get rid of the bridge onramp and off-ramp on River and redevelop that section of River to Division Street. Do some damn archaeology. Matthias and Jacob Vanderheyden's homes are there for the exposing (remember them, two of the three founders of Troy?). I would like to build a replica of the USS Monitor and have it moored on the river. Just a few ideas off the top.

Be creative: https://web.archive.org/web/20200516220710/https://blog.timesunion.com/rittner/exploring-underutilized-tunnels-subways-alleys-and-other-cool-spaces/5189/

## Albany?

Without rehashing all the proposals I have made over the last twenty years just read about them now. Why not try my Albany Historium or the Rittner-Wolcott Albany Plan of Preservation of 2000, or The Albany Greenbelt of 1984. How about excavating the remaining portion of Fort Albany on Broadway and turning it into a tourist trap? Or even the original Fort Nassau. Take unique places in the city and spiff them up. Be creative (https://web.archive.org/web/20200516220710/https://blog.timesunion.com/rittner/exploring-underutilized-tunnels-subways-alleys-and-other-cool-spaces/5189/).

You already gave up any Dutch history you had. You lost the Half Moon and didn't even get the Onrust. How stupid. You tore down your Dutch History and even had a teenager admonish you in a poem in 1835 for doing it!! That was 185 years ago! Lesson not learned! There is part of a Dutch House left at 48 Hudson. Help Historic Albany Foundation restore it.

Photograph every building, do a historic inventory of the remaining historic structures and compile a searchable database and add individual histories that anyone can explore. In Albany you have a head start. I created an antebellum building inventory a few years ago for Historic Albany Foundation. Use that for starters. Start preventing continuous demolition by neglect.

## Schenectady

Oh brother. You just tore down the oldest buildings outside the Stockade on State Street and put up modern crap that looks like everything else going up in the Capital District. What is it with you guys? Are you all sharing the same CAD program? You just destroyed any vestige of one of the most important military roads west, the original road to Van Velson's mill, the Westinghouse home sites, etc. Metrowreck has total power it seems to destroy Schenectady's remaining historic sites unabated.
Fix the Stockade. You need a gyroscope trying to navigate the sidewalks. Keep the original slate and bluestone but at least straighten them out. Bury the wires and bring back the original character of the original village. And ignore the loud mouths.
If you haven't already make the Woodlawn Pine Bush Preserve Forever wild, you know, like you said you would years ago?

Photograph every building, do a historic inventory of the remaining historic structures and compile a searchable database and add individual histories that anyone can explore. When I was the city and county historian I created a countywide database. It's a start.

You built a new train station and there is nothing in it talking about the importance of Schenectady having the first continuous passenger railroad in America, or the fact that it was the railroad hub during the 19th century with several railroads go every direction before 1850?

I wish I had more but you already destroyed most of your history.

## FOR THE ENTIRE CAPITAL DISTRICT

Photograph every building in Troy, Albany and Schenectady and create a database with their histories.

Hire some photographers and compile a photographic history of the daily life in the Capital District for a time capsule. Create a coordinated arts council and finance it so local artists can create murals and artworks throughout the area.

Create a job bank of historic artisans. Teach men and women how to do historic plasterwork, make wrought and cast iron, historic brick laying and repointing, and other artisan historic building techniques that homeowners of historic buildings can hire to restore their homes authentically.

Utilize these talents to help all the local historical societies that maintain historic buildings or museums. Every one of them that I have visited has falling plaster, leaks, foundation problems, plaster falling, etc. Non-profits are barely holding on as it is with very little money for this kind of upkeep.

Free sidewalk program where properly trained artisans can repave all the sidewalks in the cities. Plant trees. Create more specialized urban parks and playgrounds. Create historic walking trails in the cities like they have in Boston and New York City, for example.

Fund youth to create documentaries and other film projects based on their neighborhoods.

The Capital District is missing out on millions of dollars in tourist money. Two of the most visited historic sites by tourists deal with railroads and the Civil War. American railroading began in Schenectady. Troy helped finance and build the USS Monitor that turned the war in favor of the North, and had the first military reconnaissance using air balloons. Schenectady built tanks and the famous M-1 tank killer in World War II, and it goes on and on. Albany invented perforated toilet paper. Ok, not every invention was monumental but the point is the Capital District should be one of the most frequent visitation sites for heritage tourists along with the other top cities like Boston, Santa Fe, Philadelphia, Charleston, Williamsburg, New Orleans, and Washington DC We have MORE history than any of those cities.

Heritage tourism is considered one of the fastest-growing segments in the industry and in 2018 was a $171 billion annual spend.

According to the American Bus Association, Eighty-one percent of US tourists are considered "cultural tourists," and 56 percent of the US population indicated it included at least one cultural, arts, historic or heritage activity or event while on a trip in the past year. Cultural tourists spend more and stay longer: Average spend is 60 percent more at approximately $1,319 per trip, as compared to $820 for the traditional, domestic leisure traveler. Cultural tourists take 3.6 trips vs. 3.4 trips annually.

Forty-one percent of cultural tourists are affluent and well-educated baby boomers. They tend to engage with locals through immersive experiences, seek to enrich their lives, and prefer leisure travel that is educational. Forty percent will pay more for distinctive lodging. Millennial are a growth market for heritage tourism, as 73 percent want to engage in a destination's arts and cultural assets, while two-thirds rated authenticity as extremely important in their travel decisions.

So what are the benefits of heritage tourism? Carolyn Childs from MyTravelResearch.com puts it in perspective.

Economic Benefits of Cultural and Heritage Tourism
- Injects new money into the economy, boosting businesses and tax revenues
- Creates new jobs, businesses, events and attractions, thus helping diversify the local economy
- Supports small businesses and enables them to expand
- Promotes the active preservation and protection of important local resources
- Builds vital relationships among and within local communities
- Helps encourage the development and maintenance of new/existing community amenities

Social Benefits of Cultural and Heritage Tourism
- Helps build social capital
- Promotes preservation of local traditions, customs and culture. UNESCO now recognizes intangible cultural heritage as being as important as buildings. A market for and traditional projects provides the economic support for keeping these skills and traditions alive
- Promotes positive behavior
- Helps improve the community's image and pride
- Promotes community beautification
- Builds opportunities for healthy and useful community relationships and partnerships
- Provides research, education and work-placement opportunities for students
- Creates enjoyable opportunities for both local residents and visitors attracted to the cultural arts, history and preservation
- Boosts local investment in heritage resources and amenities that support tourism services
- 

These are just a few ideas that probably will never happen. We live in the oldest historic continuously settled community in America and history has shown that those in elected positions couldn't care less. Not one of them over the course of the last 50 years has put together a program to recognize this history. Most have talked the talk, but fallen flat on their face when it came to the walk.

The only thing worse than an ignorance of history is a willingness to show it.

Governor DeWitt Clinton, 1825-1828. Painting by Rembrandt Peale.

# Welcome to Albany's Renaissance (Hotel)
First Published on October 21, 2015 R 9:56 pm

**History of the former DeWitt Clinton Hotel**

Joe Nicolla and Marriott Corporation are heroes in my book. They have teamed up to bring back one of Albany's most illustrious hotels, the former DeWitt Clinton at the corner of Eagle and State Streets. What they have done is remarkable. They have retained the major historic elements of this hotel but in fact made it a new state of the art modern hotel. The Renaissance brand is one of their highest levels of comfort and no one will be disappointed. Before we discuss the "new" hotel, let's delve into the memorable history of its earlier glory days.

The Dewitt Clinton Hotel was built in 1926-27 and opened in August 1927 two years

Site of the DeWitt Clinton was two former 19th century mansions.

before the Great Depression of 1929. While the first to sign the registry was Governor Al Smith, the actual first sleepover was by Dewitt Clinton, Jr., a feral black and white kitten who wandered into the hotel in August and made itself comfortable in a fourth floor bedroom. The kitten left on August 30 after giving up its room for a basket under the lobby desk, no doubt angry about its reduced service. I have

Alfred Birch Huested, druggist.

suggested to Marriott that they get one for a mascot in the lobby.

The Dewitt Clinton became the hotel of choice by nearby legislators of the Democratic Party who found the hotel convenient for its excellent rooms, service, and minute walk to the Capitol. Many a political deal was made at the hotel's restaurant and bar until it closed in 1975.

After Albany began moving up the hill in the middle of the 19th century, former mansions were converted to apartment buildings and hotels, and also later converted to commercial use. Many were remodeled with new facades, additional floors added, and expansions in the back. Before the Dewitt Clinton Hotel was built in 1926, Number 144 and 142 State Street were typical mansions of the times. Number 144, on the corner of State and Eagle, was called The Holland Flats and the first floor was converted to a drug store operated by Alfred Birch Huested & Company. Huested was a graduate of Albany Medical College and started his business in 1868. He and his partner G. V. Dillenback, who joined in 1886, occupied the first floor and basement. Huested was a Civil War veteran, a surgeon to the 2nd NY Calvary. He was part of the regiment that guarded the Overland Stage route in 1866. He was president of the State Board of Pharmacy, professor of Botany at Albany College of Pharmacy, and one of the founders of the NYS Pharmaceutical Association. He retired from the business in 1909. The drug store moved a

Notice of hotel building construction on the front of 142 State Street These two mansions made way for the DeWitt The Albany County Jail and later hospital can be seen in the back.

Mayor Franklin Townsend.

few doors down street and then to Broadway and went bankrupt in 1964 after serving Albany for 99 years.

The Flats had as renter's doctors such as Willis G. MacDonald, S. O. Vanderpool and such politicians as banker and Albany Mayor Franklin Townsend (who was born at 146 State), Assemblyman James W. Huested, and County Fuel Administrator Guy D. Hills.

Number 142 State became a boarding house owned by E. H. Pierce in 1907. These two buildings were demolished and replaced in 1926 by the Dewitt Clinton Hotel.

The DeWitt Clinton Hotel was first made public in June 1926, but not as the DeWitt Clinton. On June 16, the local papers wrote that: *"Construction of an eleven story hotel on the east side of Eagle Street from State to Howard Streets to be known as the Albany Metropolitan Hotel was assured yesterday with the announcement that S. W. Straus and company of NYC has agreed to underwrite the first issue of 6 1.4% first mortgage gold bonds to the amount of $1,800,000."* A few days later on the 23rd the paper advertised that bonds to build the "Albany Metropolitan Hotel" as it was called for $1,800,000 would be sold. The hotel would be *"ten stories high containing 405 rooms and 405 baths to be erected on the entire block front on the east side of Eagle Street between State and Howard."* They go on to say the reason for the need for a hotel is, *"Albany suffers from an acute shortage of hotel accommodations, governmental legislative and court activities during the winter and heavy automobile traffic during summer secure the success of the hotel."*

Knott Hotel advertisement for their NYC hotels.

159

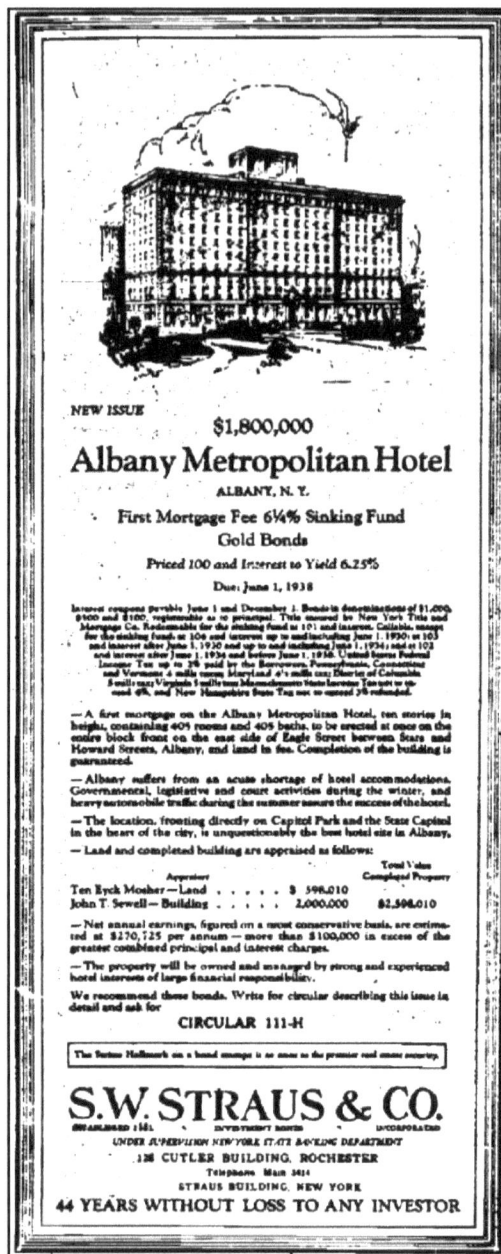

June 26, 1926, announcement.

The Metropolitan Realty, Inc., a holding company in NYC was the project originator and was made up of Darwin R. James, President of the East River Savings Bank; A. E. Lefcouret, Manhattan realty owner and operator; Edward A. Keeler, president of Keeler, Inc., Manhattan; Augustus P. Loring and William J. McDonald and Alexander Whiteside of Boston, Mass. David H. Knott, Former sheriff of New York County, was president of the operating company.

It was Knott who belonged to a family that ran one of the oldest hotel chains in the country, the Knott Hotel Corporation. It was the Knott Corporation that would run the Albany Metropolitan Hotel.

The Albany hotel was going to be the start of a national hotel chain. On June 27, 1926, a newspaper wrote: *"The Albany Metropolitan Hotel, first unit of a national chain of large modern hotels involving an investment of $25,000,000 or more, will immediately be erected on a full block frontage at State, Eagle and Howard St., Albany NY. It will cost about $3,000,000. The chain of other Metropolitan Hotels will be extended to Boston, Baltimore and possible New York. A site for the Boston metropolitan has been purchased at the cottage farms bridge over the Charles River."*

The project got off on shaky grounds though when it was rumored on November 27, 1926, that Knott *"had abandoned their plans to operate the Albany Metropolitan and the Admiral,"* another hotel that was going to be built called the Admiral in Albany. Knott denied the rumor and said they would operate both hotels. Contracts were awarded on January 10, 1927, aggregating more than $200,000 for the plumbing work to E. T. Doyle and Son, Inc. of Albany. On January 22, the National Hotel Review wrote that the Hotel Admiral Albany was renamed Hotel Hackett.

*"The new hotel construction at Maiden Lane and James Street, Albany NY which is to be operated by the Knott chain and which has hitherto been known as the Hotel Admiral has been renamed the Hotel Hackett, to honor the memory of the late Mayor William S. Hackett of that city. The change was made in accordance with the personal request of Governor Alfred E. Smith, of NY and Mayor John Boyd Thacher of Albany. Both presented the suggestion to David H. Knott, head of the Knott organization, and to S. F. Wheeler, president of the Mortgage Clearing Company, who readily consented. Mr. Wheeler, who made the announcement of the change of name, said this week that foundations of the Hackett have been completed and that the erection of the steelwork is awaiting the arrival of materials."*

There was a lawsuit over the Hackett and it was never built.

The DeWitt Clinton was designed by noted Houston architect Kenneth Franzheim. His bio from the University of Houston lists many of his accomplishments.

### KENNETH FRANZHEIM, *(1890–1959).*

Noted architect of the DeWitt Clinton, Kenneth Franzheim.

*Kenneth Franzheim, architect, was born on October 28, 1890, in Wheeling, West Virginia, the son of Charles W. and Lida Riddle (Merts) Franzheim. He graduated from Lawrenceville School and Massachusetts Institute of Technology (B. A. 1913), then worked from 1913 until 1917 for the Boston architect Welles Bosworth. He subsequently served for two years at Ellington Field outside Houston, Texas, as a first flight lieutenant in the United States Army Air Corps. On May 12, 1919, he married Elizabeth Frances Simms; they had three children, one of whom, Kenneth Franzheim II, served as ambassador to New Zealand, Western Samoa, Fiji, and Tonga during President Richard M. Nixon's administration.*

*Franzheim became a partner of the Detroit architect C. Howard Crane in 1920. He worked for Crane in Chicago, then in Boston. In 1925 he began independent practice in New York, where he*

DEWITT CLINTON HOTEL, ALBANY, N. Y.

A photograph of the opening of the DeWitt Clinton by Franzheim and included in his portfolio of work.

*specialized in the design of large commercial buildings and airports. He was retained in 1928 by Jesse H. Jones to collaborate with Alfred C. Finn on the design of the thirty-seven-story Gulf Building, Houston (1929), and to design a temporary coliseum for the Democratic national convention in Houston. Also for Jones, Franzheim designed a forty-two-story office building (1930) and a twenty-story apartment building (1931) in midtown Manhattan. A second round of major projects in Houston, undertaken with John F. Staub, led Franzheim to move his practice from New York to Houston in 1937, although he maintained a New York office until 1940. From 1941 until 1944 Franzheim worked in Washington, D.C. Upon returning to Houston he established himself as the foremost commercial architect in the city, a position he held until his death. Most of the buildings that he produced in Houston were examples of modernistic architecture. Ben A. Dore, another former partner of C. Howard Crane, was his chief designer.*

*Franzheim's major buildings in Houston were the seventeen-story Humble Tower (1936, with Staub); the second Hermann Hospital and the Hermann Professional Building (1949, with Hedrick and Lindsley); the eighteen-story Prudential Building (1952); the twenty-one-story Texas National Bank building (1955); and the twenty-four-story Bank of the Southwest building (1956).*

*Franzheim was also responsible for the twenty-one-story National Bank of Commerce building in San Antonio (1957, with Atlee B. and Robert M. Ayres. Franzheim's best known Houston building was Foley's Department Store (1947, 1957)), for which he won an Award of Merit from the American Institute of Architects in 1950.*

*Franzheim was particularly interested in incorporating works of art in his architecture, and this led to collaboration with the artists Wheeler Williams, Peter Hurd, Leo Friedlander, and Rufino Tamayo. Franzheim was the first chairman of the board of the Allied Arts Association of Houston and was an honorary member of the National Sculpture Society. In 1949 he was elected to fellowship in the American Institute of Architects, the same year that he served as chairman of the institute's annual convention, which was held in Houston, and as president of the Houston Chapter of the AIA. Franzheim also was an honorary member of the Mexican Society of Architects; after 1945 he maintained a second home in Mexico City. He was a member and deacon of the First Presbyterian Church of Houston. He belonged to the Bayou Club, the Houston Country Club, the Coronado Club, and the Ramada Club. Franzheim died in Mexico on March 13, 1959, and is buried in Glenwood Cemetery, Houston.*

Franzheim had gone independent in 1925 and the Dewitt Clinton would have been one of his first individual works. Considering how famous he became later, the DeWitt Clinton is considered an important part of his life work.

The Albany Metropolitan Corporation, with Russell D. Engs, president, was now in charge of building the Albany Metropolitan Hotel (DeWitt Clinton) and announced on May 17, 1927, that it should be opened for business by Labor Day. However a few lawsuits followed that statement. On July 7, 1927, Gasper Michaud of 20 Willow Street, Cohoes was awarded $10.69 from a hearing at the Workmen's Compensation court. On November 26, they were sued for $67,239.32 for damages by E. W. Tompkins stating they violated the contract to install a heating and ventilating system in the hotel. On February 17, 1928, attorney William R. Daniels from Buffalo was in Albany to file a mechanic's lien *"against the new DeWitt Clinton hotel that opened here under the ownership of the Albany Metropolitan Corporation."* It was for $6600 owed to the Italian Mosaic and Marble Company of Buffalo.

The Hotel did open and was operated by the Knott Hotel Corporation for most of its existence. During the life of the hotel several members of the Knott family died. On October 26, 1951, William J. Nott, 69 died. His obit read:

*"President and general manager of Knott Hotels corporate, one of the largest and oldest hotel chains in the country died in North Country community hospital in Glen Cove, LI. Born in Washington*

*Square of NYC and educated at private schools. He entered the business which his parents James and Margaret Knott found and directed in the 1920s he became the active head of the business which his brother David former sheriff of NY county is board chairman. In 1927 when the corporation was formed he was named president."*

Unfortunately his brother David who organized the building of the DeWitt died just three years later. On May 5, 1954, His obit read:

*David H. Knott died. (1879-1954) "Chairman of Knott Hotels Corp of 575 Madison ave and chairman of the NY county democratic committee for 35 years. He was 75. Former Sheriff of New York County, and close friend of Governor Alfred E. Smith who later success at sheriff in 1918. He was a member of state assembly from the 25 districts in 1913. As chairman he operated 21 hotels and 8 cafeterias. He was in charge of management of the Dewitt and 34 other hotels."*

It was not a surprise that the DeWitt Clinton became the Democrat Hotel of choice since David Knott led the county Democratic Party in New York County for 35 years.

In 1958 the Knott Corporation sold the DeWitt Clinton to the Manger Hotel Corporation in January 1958 for $2 million. Manger goes back to 1906 and was known as the Wolcott Operating Company, run by Julius and William Manger who operated under the name Manger Hotels. In February plans were made to drop the name of the hotel according to Julius Manger, Jr., chairman of the board of the Manger Hotel Corporation. The newspaper reported: *"For a brief time it will be called the Manger Dewitt Clinton and then it will become the Manger Hotel."* They added a restaurant specializing in charcoal broiled steaks. Other improvements considered were free parking for guests and patrons, renovating the second floor to provide a Purple Tree Cocktail Lounge similar to those in five of the 11 hotels of the Manger chain. These rooms with soft lighting and deep carpets featured a plastic tree which lights up in a purplish glow when bathes in "Black light." Also planned was an enlargement of the hotel's banquet and convention facilities. Also long time manager John J. Hyland was succeeded by Charles J. Mack who managed their hotel in Grand Rapids, Michigan. Hyland was manager of the Dewitt since 1928.

Manger held on to it until July 8, 1963, when they sold it back to Knott. During the Manger period they had their own coffee brand, Manger Hotels Columbian Coffee, and sponsored a TV show, Open End, over WNTA-TV in New York. They sponsored a portion of the David Susskind panel show.

### 'Open End' satire used to push coffee sales

Another premium-priced coffee is taking to the air, this one with a "discussion show." Manger Hotels Coffee signed on as a sponsor of *Open End* last night (Jan. 8) over WNTA-TV New York with its own free-for-all titled "Either End." Adaptations of the commercial satire will be used in spot, distribution to be pushed forth nationally from markets where Manger's 14 hotels are located. A planned radio campaign may use a modified version of "Either End."

Copy for Manger Hotels, a brand that dates back to 1906, was prepared by the Wexton Co., New York. One point made is the product's Colombian content, taking advantage of a million-dollar tv spot campaign by the National Federation of Coffee Growers of Colombia (placed by Doyle Dane Bernbach, New York).

To make its satirical (and serious-selling) points, "Either End" is done in a kind of stop-motion camera technique. Dialogue is synchronized to dozens of still shots that show comic panels discussing, disputing and drinking coffee.

Manger Hotels Coffee sponsors the 11-11:30 p.m. portion of the David Susskind panel show programmed by WNTA-TV Sundays, 10 p.m. to conclusion. The advertiser also has ordered morning time on WNBC-TV New York and will start in other markets on a schedule still to be announced.

At a production session one of the "Either End" actors cues a scene that focusses on byplay between "Sylvia Spivak (!), eminent divorce lawyer," and the bored "Prof. Hickman Brood, marriage counselor" (yawning). "Moderator" at left warms up for the scene with a Susskind-like gesture as "Dr. Frank Bailey, author of 'Children Are No Excuse,'" delays his characterization to identify the shot. The resulting take shows conflicting reactions to a discussion of "Marriage and love: do they really go together?" Conflict is brewing not only over the marriage question but over one panelist's refusal to drink coffee.

During the Manger period they had their own coffee brand, Manger Hotels Columbian Coffee, and sponsored a TV show, Open End, over WNTA-TV in New York. They sponsored a portion of the David Susskind panel show.

On September 26, 1967, David H. Knott was elected director of Knott Hotels Corp. He was the great grandson of James Knott and his wife, founders, and son of David Knott. Knott was the oldest hotel management organization in the country. His position was director of the real estate division.

The following year on October 11, 1968, Daniel C. Hickey was elected president of the board of Knott Hotels. He was formerly the president of the Hotel Association of New York City. He succeeded Willard E. Dodd who retired. Dodd was with the company for 40 years and president for the last fifteen.

Hickey became president of the hotel association in 1964. He started in the business in 1938 at the Hotel Commodore later becoming president of that hotel and of the Zeckerndorf Hotels Corp.

On April 23, 1989, James Knott, 79 died of bone cancer. He was the former chairman of Knott Hotels Corporation. He joined Knott in 1933 and became chairman of the board in 1954 and was the last Knott to own the company until it was sold to Trusthouse Forte Hotels in 1977 shortly after the closing of the DeWitt Clinton.

The DeWitt Hotel nevertheless had a soft opening in 1927.

One of the earliest and more famous hotel guests took place on March 1, 1928. Charles Lindberg and Lt. Lester J. Maitland USA who with LT. Albert F. Hegenberger was the first to span the dreary stretch of waters that separate the golden gate from Hawaii appeared before the joint session of senate and assembly to advocate uniform regulation of aerial traffic.

Lindbergh was put up on the 11th floor of the Dewitt Clinton with his party and some of the visiting airmen. He left later to see then Governor Alfred E. Smith.

Also that year the hotel started to broadcast big band music over WGY the second radio station created in New York State. Dinner music was broadcast on Thursdays. On May 28, 1928, The German Irish fliers of the Bemen were guest of the city and had the same suite at the Dewitt that Lindbergh had the previous March. They went to the hotel from train car at 9 AM and stayed at Dewitt for breakfast and reception till 12:40 when the governor and his son appeared. 10,000 Albanians cheered the fliers as they rode the Union Station to the hotel.

The Hotel became known as the "Democrat's Hotel" while the nearby Ten Eyck Hotel on North Pearl Street just a block and half down from the Dewitt was known as the "Republican's Hotel." Until the DeWitt closed in 1975 many a political deal was made in the bar and restaurant and rooms that many of them lived in during the legislative years.

Here is a sample of the politics over the decades:

**1920's**

1928 Dec 2
Alfred E. Smith lived at the Dewitt for some time after he goes out of office on Jan 1.

1929 Mar 14
Former Gov. Al Smith was confined to his apartment at the Dewitt Clinton with a sore throat.

**1930's**

1932 Oct 3

Two gubernatorial hopefuls opened headquarters, Colonel Lehman at the Dewitt and Mayor Thacher at the Hotel Ten Eyck

1939 June 7

New Bribe of $1,750 charged to Moran by taxi operator

General session trial of Edward S. Moran, Jr., former Brooklyn assemblyman in the alleged acceptance of 36k in bribes in 1936 from the heads of two taxicab companies. The bribes that Burge M. Seymour, president of the Terminal Systems gave 20k to Seymour for an unidentified legislator. Levin Rank president of the Parmelee Transportation Company said he had sent 20k for backing legislation favorable to the taxi company and gave the defendant either 2k or $1,750 to the defendant in the Dewitt Clinton on the evening of Feb. 25, 1936.

1933 Jan 2

Governor Lehman was staying at the DeWitt before he went to governor's mansion.

**1940's**

1948 Apr 3

Gov. Herbert H. Lehman spoke at the opening session of the state convention of the Americans for Democratic Action at the Dewitt.

1946 Nov 28

Members of the associated press in NY were advised that the annual state meeting would be held Dec 16 at the Dewitt. Governor Dewy has agreed to address the evening session. Lt Gov. Joe R. Hanley also to speak.

1946

Albany boss Dan O'Connell had a suite. Saturday Evening Post was doing a series on America cities and this issue was going to be on Albany but not favorable so he had his henchmen buy every copy in every newsroom so no one could read it. A cleaning lady seeing the issues in his office stole one. A local historian has that copy.

1946 August 29

Fala the dog had the red rug rolled for the collie and his mistress Mrs. Eleanor Roosevelt at the Dewitt. They checked in for the democratic state convention. Mrs.

Roosevelt is the convention keynoted. The dog and Roosevelt was excluded from a Maine hotel. The manager of the Dewitt said: *"Fala is an old friend of ours. We'll even lay in a special supply of dog biscuit."*

1946 March 6
Judge G. Z. Medalie died of acute bronchitis, Associate Judge of the Court of Appeals and political godfather of governor Dewey. He died at 5:10 AM at the Dewitt in his room. Dewey orders flags half staffed.

1944
Elliott V. Bell NYS Superintendent of Banks became head of Dewey's policymaking and speech writing staff, which was installed on two floors of the Albany's Dewitt Clinton Hotel. John Burton the state budget director was put in charge of research.

1944 Jan 5
Benjamin F. Feinberg of Plattsburgh was selected as republican majority leader and president pro tempore of the state senate after a bitter battle. There were 30 republicans senators taking part in the conference that was held in the dining room of the Dewitt and every effort was made to keep the struggle that went on behind the scenes from becoming known, and the fact that they were in the Dems hotel!

1942 Feb 8
Gov. Herbert H. Lehman spoke at a two-day conference to formulate the legislative program of the NY League of Women Voters. They met at the Dewitt at the luncheon. Speakers included the governor and Ms. Margaret bondfield, a former Minister of Labor in the British Cabinet.

1940 Dec 17
Some 47 electors of NYS cast their ballots for president Roosevelt today in the senate chamber, they also voted to donate their salaries, $15 a day each and mileage to the Georgia Warm Springs Foundation. They had a luncheon at the Dewitt with Secretary of State Walsh.

**1950's**

1955 Mar 19
Attorney general Jacob Javitts at a luncheon at Dewitt brought together 125 assistant attorneys general, chief investigators, record clerks, finance offers and administration supervisors of the department main office around the state to discuses department

polices and organizations. Idea was to be "alert for complaints" of state law violations.

1953 Jan 6
Pre session caucus at the Dewitt led to an agreement among NYC Dem leaders clearing the way for selection of assemblyman Eugene F. Bannigan of Brooklyn and Senator Francis J. Mahoney of Manhattan as minority leaders of the 1953 legislature.

1952 Feb 10
Women's division of the democrat state committee would meet Feb. 18 at the Dewitt to discuss state and national issues.

## 1960's

1966, May 11
Howard J. Samuels entered the fight for the Dem nomination for governor with attack on Rockefeller at a luncheon at the Dewitt.

1966 Jan 19
NYC mayor Lindsey stole the show on budget day as it was introduced, the press was more interested in John V. Lindsay making his first trip to Albany. Rockefeller explained, as he was an hour late to address the annual legislative meeting for the state association for mental health at the Dewitt Clinton.

1965 Dec 17
Dem leaders Senator Joseph Zaretzki and Assembly speaker Anthony J. Travia, and again booked rooms at the Dewitt.

1965 Jan 22
Mayor Wagner declared that his sole motive in accusing the democrat state chairman of attempted bribery was to prevent the use of money to settle the leadership fight in the legislature. The bribe meeting took place at the Dewitt on Jan 12.

1965 Jan 19
Mayor Wagner of NYC named J. Raymond Jones leader of the NY County Dem organization as the person whom alleged bribe offers were paid to influence the outcome of the leadership battle in the legislature. The bribe was in the form of expense funds to two senators made at a meeting in the Dewitt Clinton, meeting was attended by six party leaders in addition to McKeon.

1964 Jan 9
Chairman of the Democratic Party organization in the states 62 counties will meet to discuss the 1964 campaign at the Dewitt.

1960
John F. Kennedy spoke at the Dewitt. Stayed there.

**1970's**

1979 Jun 6
202nd session of legislature ending quiet.

Assembly speaker Stanley Fink commented on the sense that no one was unhappy that the session was closing down:

*"I am getting the sense that nobody is unhappy that we're getting ready to close down." It is, after all, hard to maintain the traditional demeanor of a salesmen's convention when the session shuffles on for six and seven months at a time."*

*"I think when they closed down the Dewitt that took a lot of that aspect out of the place," It used to be you could relive each day's activities in the lobby – Republicans at the Ten Eyck, Democrats at the Dewitt. Now people are scattered. They're not together anymore and it's different."*

Article goes on to say that George Chelius restored the old hotel nightclub with plush red velvet chairs and the original glass floor that reputedly was danced on by Elizabeth Taylor the night she married Nicky Hilton in 1950 and the infamous Legs Diamond in the 1930s.

1975 March 17
Women's caucus ends on cheering note

Bella for Senator, Krupsak for Governor, the convention of NYS Women's Political Caucus came to a close with nearly 200 women rose to their feet and cheered their two member favorites, Representative Bella S. Abzug and Lt. Gov. Mary Ann Krupsak. They spoke to the women in the ballroom at the Dewitt.

1975, Jan 30
According to a local newspaper article many legislators lived in the hotel and frequented the nearby Ambassador Bar or the one in the Dewitt.

1975 Jan 8
Stanley Steingut becomes speaker of assembly. Pre session caucus at the Dewitt Clinton

1974 Mar 5
Governor Wilson and leaders, 800 of them, gathered for the 1974 legislative conference of the state AFLC CIO. They spoke at the Dewitt capacity crowed.

1970
Bronx Democrat, Seymour Posner had a room at the hotel. Harvey Strelzin, from Brooklyn, and Stanley Steingut, Assembly minority leader in 1970 had a suite at the hotel.

1970 Dec 17
The mayors of the states six largest cities (Albany, Syracuse, Buffalo, New York, Rochester and Yonkers.) met with Rockefeller to get more funds and the governor told them *"the state is in the same boat as they are"* at the Dewitt. Before they met with the Governor they discussed their fiscal problems at the hotel.

1970 Dec 6
Howard J. Samuels urged the Democratic State Committee to assert its role as the party governing body at a talk at the Dewitt Clinton.

## OTHER NOTABLE AND INTERESTING EVENTS AND TIDBITS

1993 Oct 31
There was an interesting article about an Albany operative in the local newspaper. Story about Charlie Torche, Albany political operative. *"He's long been a kind of institution in Albany, an interesting, colorful character who is one of the last vestiges of old-fashioned politics in Albany,"* said Gov. Mario M. Cuomo, who has known Torche since 1956, when Cuomo was a law clerk in the state Court of Appeals.

But Torche, retired two years ago as a lobbyist, lawyer and political gadfly, was once on a first-name basis with everyone who was anyone around Albany, a fixture at the Capitol and every gin mill within a two-mile radius.

There's a plaque on his wall from the fellows at the bar of the DeWitt Clinton Hotel, base for the Democratic legislators in years gone by and Torche's second home. It's the "Man of the Ear Award" presented Feb. 27, 1977. The verse says,

*"An Ear To The Ground/*
*His Stories Abound/*
*With Rumor and Spice/*
*And even A Slice/*
*Of Humor Befitting a Clown."*

1963 July 8
Knott buys back Dewitt from Manger

1961 Jan 9
Manger Hotels had their own brand of coffee, Manger Hotels Columbian Coffee and sponsored a TV show, Open End, over WNTA-TV in New York. Manger goes back to 1906. They sponsored a potion of the David Susskind panel show.

1960 Nov 21
Although gross operating receipts for Knott Hotel climbed in the first nine months of 1960, higher operating expenses caused a dip in net operating income.

1958, Feb 22
Knott sold the Dewitt Clinton to Manger Hotel Chain.

1958 Feb 7
Plans were made to drop the name of the hotel according to Julius Manger, Jr., chairman of the board of the Manger Hotel Corporation. For a brief time it will be called the Manger Dewitt Clinton and then it will become the Manger Hotel. They added a restaurant specializing in charcoal broiled steaks. Other improvements considered were free parking for guests and patrons, renovating the second floor to provide a Purple Tree Cocktail Lounge similar to those in five of the 11 hotels of the Manger chain. These rooms with soft lighting and deep carpets feature a plastic tree which lights up in a purplish glow when bathes in "Black light." Also enlargement of the hotel's banquet and convention facilities. Also John J. Hyland manager was succeeded by Charles J. Mack who managed their hotel in Grand Rapids, Michigan. Hyland was manager of the Dewitt since 1928.

1958, Jan 12
Manger Hotels purchased the 400 rooms Dewitt Clinton took over operations on Feb 1. Bought from Knott Hotel Corp, which built the Dewitt Clinton in 1929. Purchase for 2 million.

1957 Mar 25
A briefing session on a forthcoming airline service investigation by the Civil Aeronautic Board will be held at the Dewitt at 1o0 Am Involved airline service to 27 NYS communities.

1957 March 18
Knott Hotels 56 gross, net set highs; profit was @$2.26 a share, against $1.51.

1954, Sept. 19
Helen D. Hoffman married John R. Casey of Schenectady and had their reception at the hotel.

1954, May 5
David H. Knott died. (1879-1954) Chairman of Knott Hotels Corp of 575 Madison Ave and chairman of the NY County democratic committee for 35 years. He was 75. Former Sheriff of NY County, and close friend of governor Alfred e smith who later success at sheriff in 1918. He was a member of state assembly from the 25 districts in 1913. As chairman he operated 21 hotels and 8 cafeterias. He was in charge of management of the Dewitt and 34 other hotels.

1955 Nov 19
$507,794 earned in 9 months as gross rises to $17,432,998.

1952 Sept 27
Executive committee of the building industry employers of NYS Will hold it fall meeting at the Dewitt. Reps from 22 of the states builders associations attended.

1949 Nov 17
15 year first mortgage fee 4-6% sinking fund bonds, dated Nov. 17, 1934, due Nov. 17 1949, Albany Metropolitan Hotel (Dewitt Clinton hotel), Eagle Street between Howard and States Street streets, Albany NY, copyright May 4, 1937.

1947 Sept 21
Robert W. Leavitt of Lake George was nominated as president of the New York State Association of Real Estate Boards.

1947 May 23
Knott Chain cleared about 360k in the first months of the years. William J. Knott president reported to meeting. Occupancy was running 100% but only 40% per in the chain were transient. The rest were rented to permanent and semi permanent guests. This year the company bought interest in the Dewitt and purchased 5017 shares of common stock for $752, 550. Payment over 3 1/2 years. They have been operating the hotel under a management agreement since 1926.

1946 Dec 16
The Commerce and Industry Association of NY opened an Albany office in the Dewitt, operations to be non-political aiming to express the views of business on matters of commerce and industry of the state and to foster the trade and welfare of NY.

1944, Feb 6
Statewide realty tax relief conference held under the sponsorship of the Owners Division of the New York State Association of Real Estate Boards.

1941, Sept 13
Glen Miller broadcast his Sunset Serenade radio program from the Dewitt in between performances at the Palace in Albany and Proctors in Schenectady.

1941, Apr 26
Campaign to raise $300,000 for Hartwick College at Oneonta and Wagner College on Staten Island when 400 members of churches in the area of Albany and the faculty of the two held a dinner meeting at the hotel.

1941 April 20
Jewish Council to meet at Dewitt, luncheon, Governor Herbert H. Lehman will address the New York State Convention of the National Council of Jewish Women in Albany.

1939, Nov 6
200 delegates of 55 ski clubs made the 18th annual meeting of the United Sates Eastern American Ski Association at the Dewitt.

1934 Oct 10
John J. Hyland, manager of the Dewitt Clinton made formal announcement this week of the opening of the Crystal Room dance season. Eddie Lane and his orchestra start off there this Saturday evening.

1937, June 19
A dividend of 10 cents a share was announced by the Knott Corporation NYC, The Dewitt Clinton Hotel of Albany is a member of the Knott group of hotels. The Albany Metropolitan Hotel Corporation holding concern for the Dewitt Clinton hotel recently reported a 1936 profit and improved prospects since the financial reorganization two years ago.

1936
Albany Metropolitan Hotel has been disposed of by reorganization under 77(b).

## TWO STRIKES AFFECT THE DEWITT CLINTON

During the 1940s the DeWitt and Ten Eyck Hotels went out on strike. The democrats obeyed the picket lines while most of the republicans did not.

The 1948 Strike

1948 March 7
Increased in pay halts Albany hotel strike. Members of two AFL unions ended strike at the ten Eyck and Dewitt. Accepted a 10% wage increase. Picket lines immediately taken out. Dewitt left their jobs on Feb. 21

1948 Feb 23
Both Dewitt and Ten Eyck were on strike, asking for 40 hour workweek instead of 48 and a 25 percent pay increase. Legislators could not find rooms and had to book at other hotels.

The 1940 Strike

1940, Mar 3
Striking employees of the Dewitt returned to work today after a 13-hour conference between union and hotel reps, brought a settlement of the 6-day walkabout.

1940 Feb. 28
Lt Governor and Mrs. Charles Poletti moved out of the Dewitt today to avoid walking through a picket line established around the hotel created by the Hotel and Restaurant employees' alliance, an AFL Affiliate. Strike since Sunday morning shifted testimonial dinner for the Lt. governor by the sons of Italy to the Ten Eyck so as not to embarrass the Lt. Governor. Several other members of the legislature moved out as well.

1940 Feb. 24
Dems' obey Albany pickets. More than 50 legislators refused to cross picket lines to occupy their usual rooms at the Dewitt and Ten Eyck. Many republicans cross the lines, but a few declined to do so.

Ten Eyck was on strike with 250 employees of the hotel and restaurant employees union local 471 and the bartenders union, local 98. Most of the republicans who occupy hotel rooms reside in Albany at the ten Eyck and few of them checked out.

The Dewitt Clinton hotel employee also seeking better wages and shorter hour struck sat norming after most of the legislators had returned to their homes for the weekend. Most of the Dems reside at the Dewitt. In addition to the legislators about 25 person employed by demos senators and assemblymen also refused to cross the lines.

## FAMOUS ARTIST DIES AT HOTEL

1943 Feb 8
William Henry Hyde, portrait painter died in the Dewitt, resided for several years, and was 84. Why he spent his last few years is a mystery.
Hyde's bio follows:

William Henry Hyde
New York 1858 – 1943 Albany, New York

William Henry Hyde studied for three seasons, 1873 to 1876, in the National Academy of Design's antique class; during the same years, he was a student at Columbia University. Despite this demonstration of his commitment to art, his father, a watch importer and amateur artist, discouraged him. On graduation from Columbia in 1877, Hyde became a stockbroker and an importer of cotton goods. He continued to draw, however, receiving criticism from his friend Albert Pinkham Ryder, whom he

William Henry Hyde.

met at the National Academy. In January 1888, Hyde resolved to go to Paris to study painting. He remained for five years, working at the Academie Julian under Gustav Boulanger and Jules-Joseph Lefebvre. He also received private instruction from Alexander Harrison in Paris.

Returning to New York in 1892, Hyde opened a portrait studio. Several years later, he married Mary B. Potter, daughter of the Episcopal bishop of New York. Although he was elected to the Society of American Artists in 1893, the same year he first exhibited in an Academy annual exhibition, Hyde found it expedient to take on considerable illustration work at Harper's and Scribner's magazines in order to support himself. Although he continued to exhibit regularly at the National Academy until 1935, showing a nearly even mix of portraits and subject pictures, little is know of his later career. He is said to have painted scenic spots throughout Minnesota in the late nineteenth century, but his principal residence remained New York, even after ill health forced him into semiretirement in the 1920s. Filling out a biographical questionnaire requested of all Academy members in 1930, Hyde made terse responses that convey a rather pessimistic evaluation of his career. For "List of honors," he noted "Not many," and for "List of important works," he wrote, "No important works."

### DEWITT CLINTON WORKER ALMOST WINS BOSTON MARATHON

1933
Dewitt cook Johnny DeGloria finished ninth in the 1933 Boston Marathon. *"At the South Framingham checkpoint, Canadian Walter Hornsby was in the lead, but DeGloria and two others were only 12 seconds behind. DeGloria remained on Hornsby's heels through Natick and Wellesley before bursting into the lead after 16 miles."*

Tim McCabe, sportswriter for the Boston Herald, wrote: *"DeGloria must have had a 25-yard lead as the turn was made at Brae Burn (Country Club on Commonwealth Avenue)."*

A few minutes later, the smaller DeGloria found himself caught and running stride-for-stride with a taller, leaner Leslie Pawson of Rhode Island. Pawson went on to win the race, while DeGloria's pace slowed. Although he eventually settled for ninth place, DeGloria crossed the finish line only steps behind Clarence DeMar, a well-known star of the day.

DeGloria remained a competitive runner the rest of his life, winning numerous area races, but he never approached the level of his brush with history in Boston in 1933.

**FAKE LETTER ASSOCIATED WITH DEWITT CLINTON**

A letter dated June 2, 1925, on letterhead of the DeWitt Clinton started: *"Dear F. Scott Fitzgerald. Thank you for you encouraging letter and your book 'The Great Gatsby." I look forward to reading it now that my own book for this year is done (are they ever really done?). Sincerely yours (signed in script) Sinclair Lewis."* This rare letter was well publicized.

A well known Los Angeles dealer offered $8500 for this note tucked in a signed, limited edition copy of Lewis' 1925 novel "Arrowsmith." Problem is the DeWitt Clinton Hotel did not exist. When exposed, the buyer had his money refunded by the dealer.

**SUICIDE ATTEMPTS**

1965 Feb 28
A 19 yr. old who was urged to jump from the top of the Dewitt Clinton on April 14 has recovered and home and back to work. Richard Reinemann, under psychiatric care at Albany Med was coasted to safety by his 7 yr. old nephew after two hours on a 36-inch wide ledge. The crowd on the on the lawn of the State Capitol had urged him to jump. "What's the matter," one teen yelled, "ya yellow?"

1956 Oct 28
Woman jumps to death. Mrs. Garnett Boisseau, 45 jumped from the 10th floor of the Dewitt. Suicide. Left two notes to her husband owner of the stable Inn at Westport and one to Dr. Thomas HaleJr., Albany Hospital.

Not all events at the DeWitt were political. The hotel was used for dinners, events, weddings and meetings by a variety of organizations.

**END OF THE DEWITT CLINTON**

After it closed in 1975, the DeWitt Clinton was renovated into senior citizen housing in 1976. It had a small fire in 1988.

**SUGGESTIONS**

Floors of the new hotel should be named in honor of some of the famous residents there. When a guest gets off the elevator an exhibit on the wall opposite can have a small history with photographs about the famous person.

If a restaurant/bar becomes part of the new hotel, a glass dance floor should be installed to celebrate the 1950 dance of Elizabeth Taylor and Nicky Hilton when they stayed there. Around the lobby there should hang various memorabilia of the old hotel, several items that I have purchased already.

**VARIOUS MEMORABILIA**

# New Renaissance Hotel Honors the History of the Old DeWitt Clinton! Restores Historic Murals!

First published on November 2, 2015 12:57 am

My last column praised the work of Joe Nicolla and Marriott Corporation for bringing back the old DeWitt Clinton Hotel back to life. One of the most important elements of the old hotel was a series of murals along the ceiling honoring major historic events that took place in New York State. If this had been a different developer and hotel chain they probably would have been destroyed them in favor of some new modern ugly whatever the trend decor is of the day. Instead Nicolla spent several thousand dollars hiring the Williamstown Art Conservation Center to come in and restore the murals. Here is the history of those murals, the artist who painted them, and a nice handy illustration that you can print out and then go visit the hotel lobby and see them in person.

## The Artist

### Muralist Victor Gerald White

Victor Gerald White (1891-1954) was born in Dublin, Ireland and moved to the United States at age 17.

He studied at the Art Students League in New York City with William Merritt Chase, Robert Henri, and George Bellows.

During World War I he served in France and was decorated as a hero for bravery. As a member of the Ambulance Corp he was cited *"for coolness, efficiency, and bravery under fire."* According to a diary by fellow soldier William Yorke Stevenson: *"He was loading two wounded men at Cappy when the Germans turned loose their shells and all the men who were helping beat it for the cellar. Vic finished the job by himself, started his car, and drove the men down out of shellfire to Cerisy."* Two of his paintings, 'Bringing the Wounded Outside Verdun with Cathedral in Background' (1916) and 'Members of the American Field Service in Village of Cappy-sur-Somme' (1914) are a result of his experiences.

He then studied art in Paris at the Academie Julian under Laurens and at the Academie de la Grande Chaumiere with Simon and Biloul.

After his return to New York he continued studying at the Art Students League in 1920 and 1926-27. He painted murals showing Cortez's adventures for a private home in 1926 and they were exhibited at the Arden Galleries in New York, the same year he was hired to paint the murals in the Dewitt Clinton Hotel in Albany. In 1930 he painted a large wall mural in the sun parlor of the Victor Morawetz Estates in Woodbury NY. In 1936 his portraits and marines were shown at the Reinhardt Galleries. His other works include murals in Wanamaker's Department store; a frieze in the Theatre Guild; a mural called The Starlight Roof in 1935 in the Waldorf-Astoria Hotel and the International Telephone and Telegraph building, both in New York City. He also had works commissioned for the Grumman Aircraft Corporation plant in Bethpage LI, and four local history panels for the post office at Rockville Center, LI (1939). The post office panels were funded by the Treasury Department Section of Painting and Sculpture, later know as The Section of Fine Arts and created in 1934 by Edward Bruce who headed the procurement division of the Treasury department. Their purpose was to decorate public buildings with high quality art for the public.

He was married to Margaret White, a portrait artist. She painted a mural of President Roosevelt for the New York Harvard Club. Victor died in Cedarhurst, LI, in 1954. His house built in 1936 in Colonial Revival style in Lawrence, NY was torn down in 2017.

**The Murals**

Mural History

When the Dewitt Clinton Hotel opened for business in 1927, the New York Historical Association published a description of the murals. These original descriptions in *italics* are followed by a more up to date explanation.

**Panel 1**

*1609.*

*Henry Hudson sails up the Grand River to the present site of Albany.*

We know today that Hudson did not make it all the way to Albany with the Half Moon but probably docked somewhere near South Bethlehem, NY. His men are reputed to have taken a small boat as far up the river as Albany.

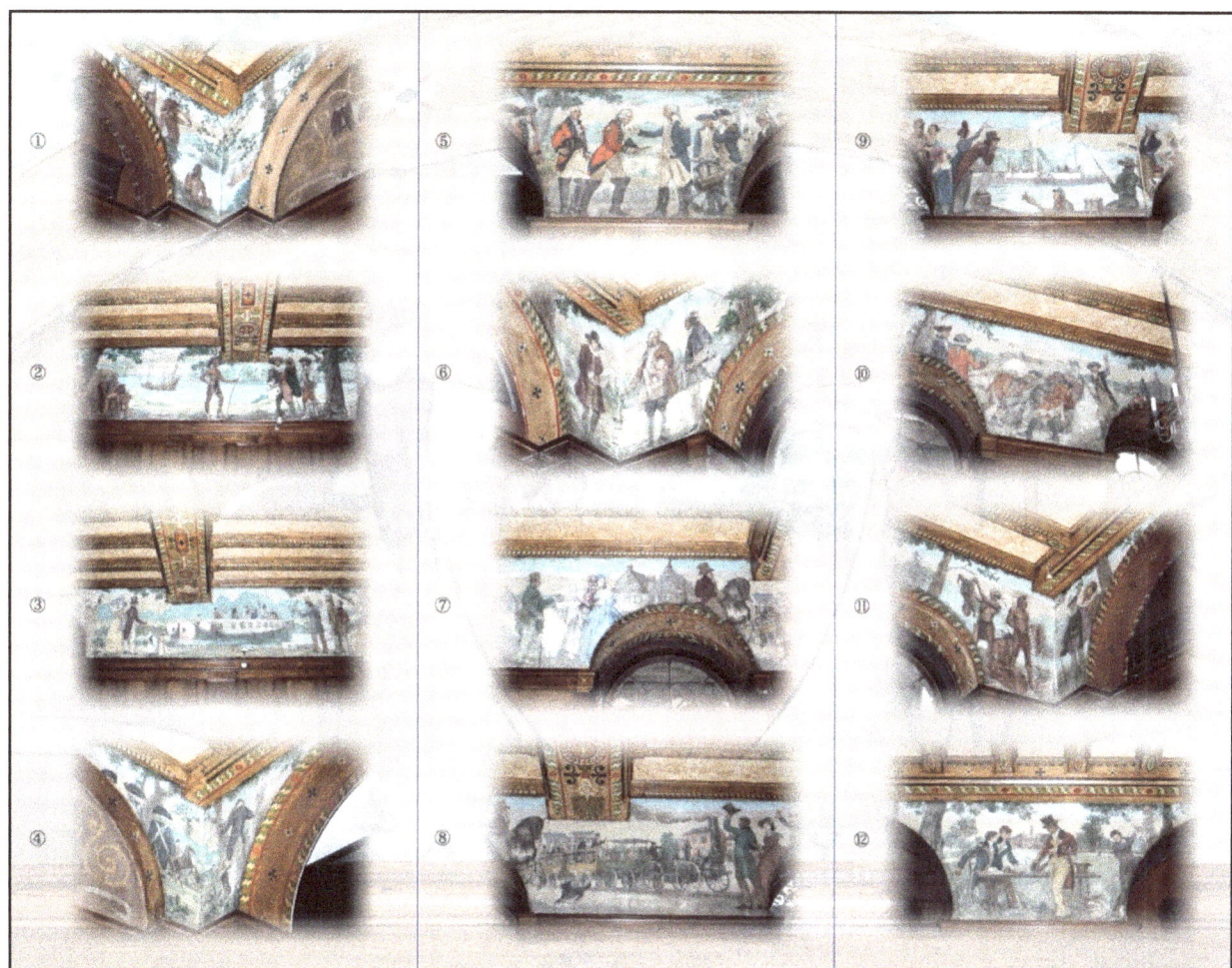

**Panel 2**

*1624.*

*Arrival off Albany of the Walloons from Holland on the "New Netherland." — entering into fur trade with the Indians.*

Eighteen Belgian families of the French speaking Walloons from the Hainaut region became the first European settlers in Albany in May 1624. The first white women was born at Fort Orange (Albany) on June 9, 1625. Sarah Rapelje was the daughter of Joris Jansen de Rapelje a Walloon, and Catelina Trico of Italian descent. It is estimated that there are one million descendants of this family alive today!

## Panel 3

*1825.*

*Erie Canal opened for its entire length with great public celebration when the "Seneca Chief" arrived at Albany with the Governor, Mayor and officials aboard - November 21. It was acclaimed all along the route and in the morning as it approached Albany its coming was made known some time before by the booming of cannon. On its reaching the Capital special services were held.*

While celebrations were taking place in Albany, a small boat from Troy, Albany's main competitor for trade, called the "Trojan Trader," and loaded with 25 tons of goods, slipped onto the canal and moved west becoming the first to conduct trade on the new canal. Albany was displeased! The two cities always competed with each other.

## Panel 4

*1777.*

*The shooting of General Fraser by Sharpshooter Timothy Murphy during the battle between General Burgoyne and General Gates. Very important event in the defeat of Burgoyne.*

Murphy lived in nearby Middleburgh, NY where he is buried and considered a hero. He was a member of Daniel Morgan's "Sharpshooter Corps" and besides Fraser he killed General Burgoyne's chief aide-de-camp Sir Francis Clerke in the same Battle at Bemis Heights at Saratoga on October 7, 1777. He eloped with the daughter of Dutch farmer Johannes Feeck to Duanesburgh and he and new wife Peggy became famous for their defense of the Middle Fort when the British raided the Schoharie Valley in 1780. The book 'The Rifleman' is based on his life.

## Panel 5

*1777.*

*General Burgoyne surrendering to General Gates at the site of Fort Hardy, Oct 17.*

The defeat after the second battle at Saratoga with Burgoyne's surrender was a turning point in the war and deciding factor in bringing France into supporting the American cause. If Burgoyne had been successful in capturing Albany, it would have cut New

England rebels off from the other colonies. After the war Burgoyne became a playwright in England.

**Panel 6**

*1686.*

*Citizens of Albany commissioned Pieter Schuyler and Robert Livingston to receive the charter from the hands of Governor Thomas Dongan of the Province of N.Y. He signed this important document on July 22, and thereupon delivered it to them.*

Albany became the longest and narrowest city in the world when the Dongan Charter gave the boundaries of Albany as 16 miles long and 1 mile wide encompassing the entire King's Highway, the major trade, transportation, and military route between the Hudson and Mohawk Valleys. This boundary description was called "The Liberty of Albany."

**Panel 7**

*1795.*

*Old Street in Albany with Old Dutch church, Penny Postman delivering letters half a century before stamps were used.*

A popular person in Albany was penny postman William B. Winne. Winne was penny postman for 48 years and died at age 90 on January 21, 1848. The first US postage stamp began on July 1, 1847. When you received your letter from Winne you paid him a penny unless the sender already paid for it.

**Panel 8**

*1831.*

*First steam passenger train in America, the DeWitt Clinton engine. Grand opening excursion September 24, from Albany to Schenectady.*

First incorporated in 1826 as the Mohawk & Hudson Railroad, the country's first steam powered passenger railroad. The Dewitt Clinton engine and several modified stage coaches as train cars made the daily trip through the Pine Bush over wooden rails until it was absorbed by the New York Central in 1853. A working replica of the Dewitt Clinton and cars can be seen at the Ford Museum in Dearborn, Michigan.

## Panel 9

*1807.*

*The first steam boat, the invention of Robert Fulton, 100 feet long with stacks 30 feet high. Left Jersey City September 4th arriving in Albany Sept. 5, making trip in 30 hours at 5 miles and hour.*

With the help of Robert Livingston, then US Ambassador to France, Fulton built 'The North River Steamboat' (later called the Clermont) the first commercial passenger boat between New York City and Albany. His final design was for the first steam driven warship *Demologos* but he died before it was built in 1815. It was renamed the *Fulton* in his honor.

## Panel 10

*1676.*

*Fort Frederick built to replace Fort Orange which was in bad condition.*

The fort, named after the son of King George II, was built on the hill atop State Street in 1676 to replace Fort Orange down on the river. Originally of wood, it was replaced by stone in 1702 and lasted until 1735 when it was dismantled and much of the stone used for the building of surrounding homes and businesses. The Southwest bastion was located just outside the entrance to the former Wellington Hotel at 136 State Street.

## Panel 11

*Trading with the Indians.*

The founding of the Albany area by the Dutch in 1614 was for the purpose of trading furs from the local indigenous nations beginning with the Mohicans and later Mohawks and others. A small fort called Fort Nassau was built on Castle Island, now Port of Albany, in 1614, under orders of Captain Adriaen Block of the trading ship Onrust.

**Panel 12**

*1829.*

*The Albany Academy with group of students, with Prof. Henry discoverer of the electric magnet.*

Joseph Henry was headed into an acting career until a friend suggested he go to the Albany Academy. Here Henry invented the electromagnet and electric motor. He also invented the doorbell, and was instrumental in the invention of the electrical telegraph which Samuel Morse expanded on and the telephone in which he helped Alexander Graham Bell. Henry created the national weather service and became the first secretary of the Smithsonian Institution. He was one of the most revered scientists of his time.

**Other Murals**

Two additional murals were painted over a doorway but do not appear to the work of White. One is the seal of Excelsior, the seal of New York State and the other is Assiduity, the Albany City seal.

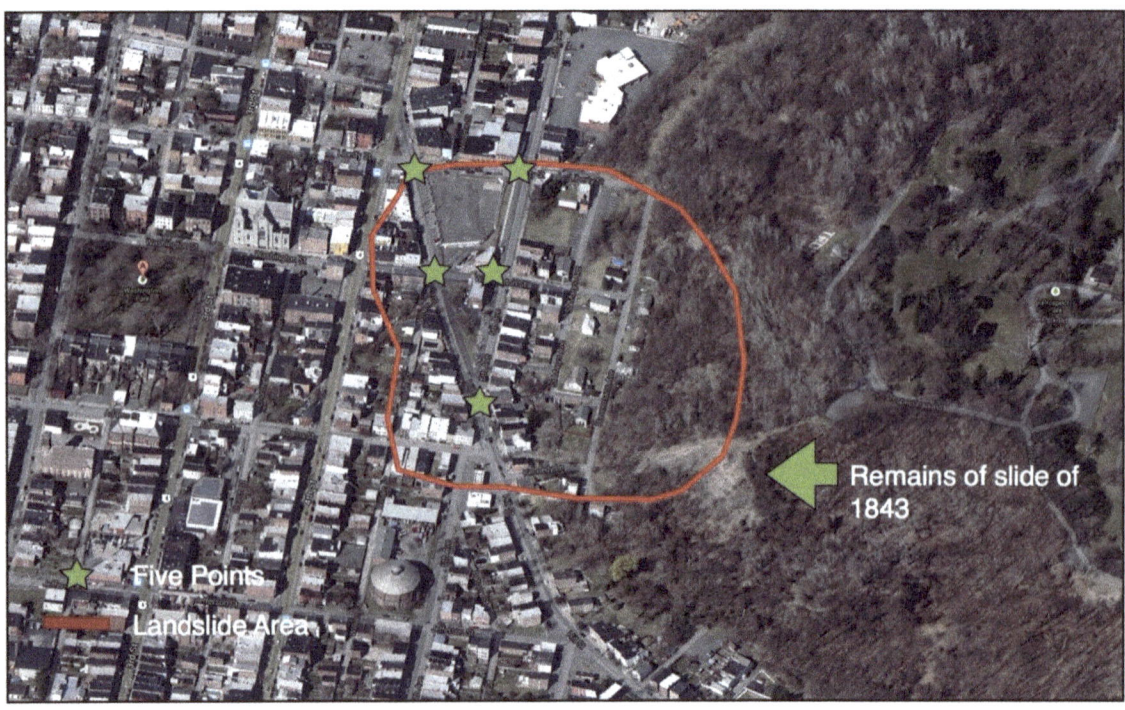

Three landslides in Troy New York in the 19th century caused deaths in 1843 and the destruction of homes and St. Peter's College on March 18, 1859.

# A Landslide of Uncommon Sense
First published on May 23, 2015 2:16 pm

The recent mudslide into the Normanskill in Bethlehem this year near the Albany Capital Hills Golf Course, owned by the City of Albany, is just another example of the lack of proper planning in the region. (See http://www.timesunion.com/news/article/Estimates-in-millions-to-fix-Normans-Kill-slide-6281229.php#photo-8030023)

This is the second major landslide in recent years on the Normanskill. This recent one in April now has a lawsuit where the golf club is accusing the town of Bethlehem for giving a permit for filling and grading on a slope well known to be unstable. Yet, according to the TU, the golf course began dumping fill before they asked for a permit.

You may remember a landslide in May 2000 along Delaware Avenue swallowed a building and shut down Delaware Avenue for a period of time. It affected many businesses and travelers. People fled their homes and businesses and some even lost food as a community garden plot disappeared. One building slid down the valley. The main fault lies in the various town boards, planning boards, and the like who fail to do their homework in the first place. Any real planner would know that way back in 1982 the New York State Geological Survey published a map and bulletin entitled "Engineering Geology Classification of the Soils of the Albany, New York 15 Minute Quadrangle."

The bulletin and map outline various geological hazards in the Capital District that includes areas that have potential for landslides, sinkhole development, wind erosion (sloughing) and flood prone areas based on the soils. The map pretty much shows the areas where landslides have occurred to have, well, landslide potential.

With this information so readily available why are houses and commercial developments allowed in these areas?

The economic impact of the 2000 landslide was in the millions. It is now estimated to cost between $1.4 and $7.8 million to "fix" the latest slide.

Where were the politicians, planning boards, environmentalists, DEC, DOT, and other agencies that supposedly have a say on regional development when roads,

Portion of geological hazards map showing much of the Normanskill to have landslide potential. Source: NYS Museum Map and Chart Series No. 36. The red dotted areas reflect landslide potential.

housing, and commercial developments are permitted on unstable soils? Seems like there is plenty of blame to go around.

# Honey, I Have a Sinking Feeling About This?
First published on October 17, 2013

You may remember last year when a man disappeared in his Florida bedroom when a large sinkhole opened up under his bed and swallowed him. While that sounded like something from a science fiction movie when it happened it is not that all rare of an event. In Florida alone between 2006 and 2010 the Florida Senate Committee on Banking and Insurance reported that insurers had received 24,671 claims for sinkhole damage. That's an average of nearly 17 claims a day, just in Florida.

The problem is based on Karst geography. Karst is the geologic term for landscapes formed mainly by the dissolving of limestone or dolomite bedrock. Those areas where large amounts of limestone or dolomite act as the bedrock are prone to sinkhole development. Groundwater is the culprit as it forms enlarged openings to form a subsurface drainage system. A mild form of carbonic acid produced from carbon dioxide in the atmosphere is responsible for the solvent power of groundwater on carbonate rocks. It literally dissolves the rock.

Sinkhole in Winter Park, Florida. Source: Internet.

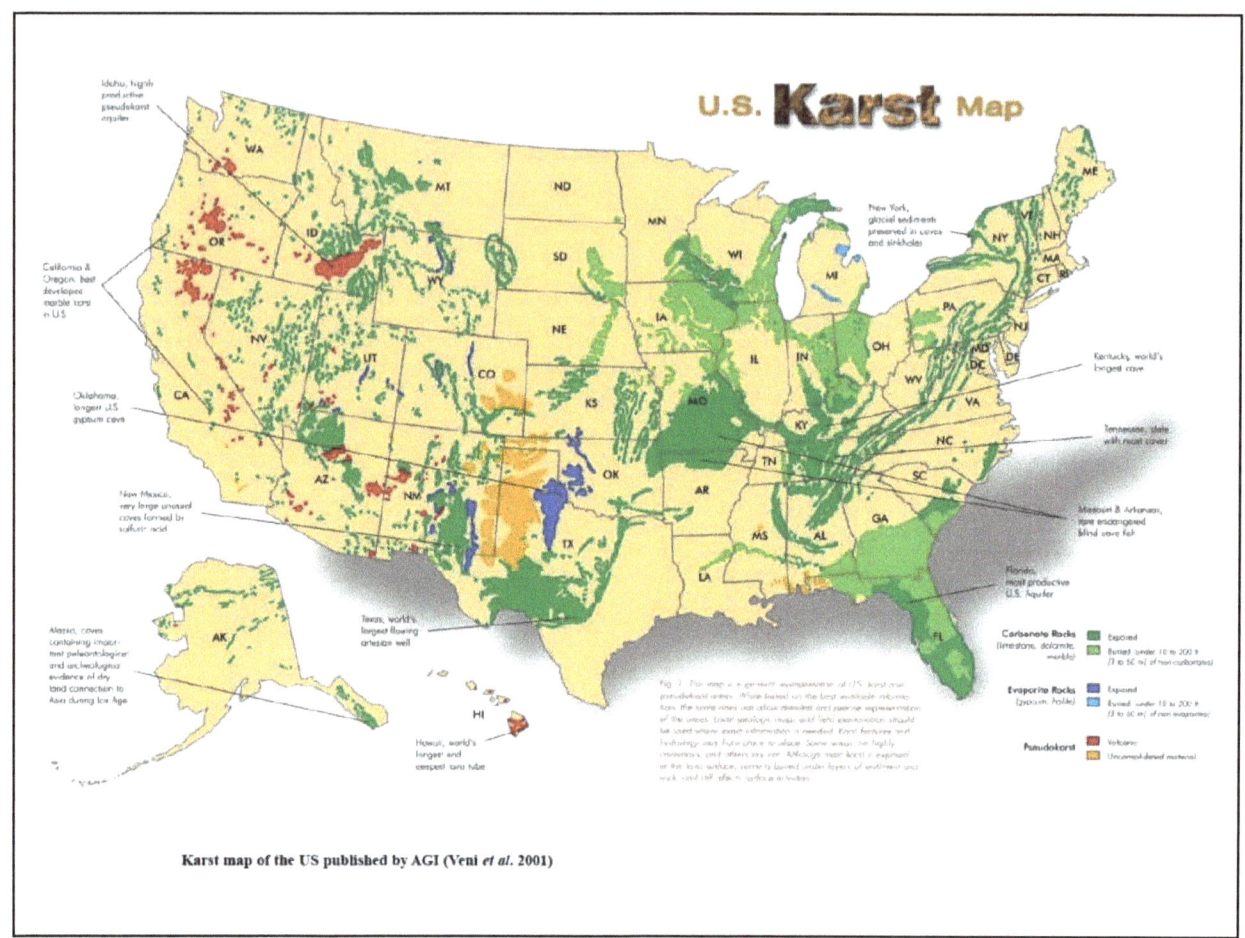

Karst Map of the US Source: Internet. AGI.

In the United States, karst underlies parts of Missouri, Arkansas, Kentucky, Tennessee, northern Alabama, Texas, and most of Florida. The entire town of Bayou Corne, Louisiana is being swallowed by a sinkhole. In Winter Park, Florida a massive sinkhole opened up very suddenly and swallowed an entire swimming pool.

Remember back in August when the Disney hotel was collapsing from a sinkhole and residents barely escaped?

New York is not immune. There are a few belts of underlaid limestone that could and do create sinkhole formation.

Not all sinkholes are caused by nature. Mankind does a good job it of as well in mining regions and where water lines erupt underground and wash away the ground. The city of Harrisburg, Pennsylvania is plagued with 40 sinkholes but they were formed from leaking old pipes. Kingston, NY had the same problem.

The Helderberg Escarpment is made up of rock types that can cause sinkholes. Photo by Don Rittner

In 2011 an 80 year old man walked out his front door in Oceanside only to fall into a sinkhole 8 feet deep. He was rescued. Troy had a big one on Lincoln Avenue this past May and Congress and 8th back in 2010. On October 16 this year people who live in Albany's Center Square neighborhood woke up to a sinkhole closing Elm Street, between Swan and Dove. I have a little one in front of my house growing each year probably from a broken water pipe but I live in Schenectady so won't hold my breath — until a car is swallowed in it.

Check out this page to see some of the largest and deadliest sinkholes here http://www.businessinsider.com/giant-sinkhole-photos-2013-3#in-november-2003-rescue-workers-had-to-remove-this-bus-with-a-crane-after-it-fell-into-a-lisbon-portugal-street-4

Locally, if you have visited Knox or Clarksville Caves you will notice they are sinkholes. Back in 1983 members of the New York State Geological Survey

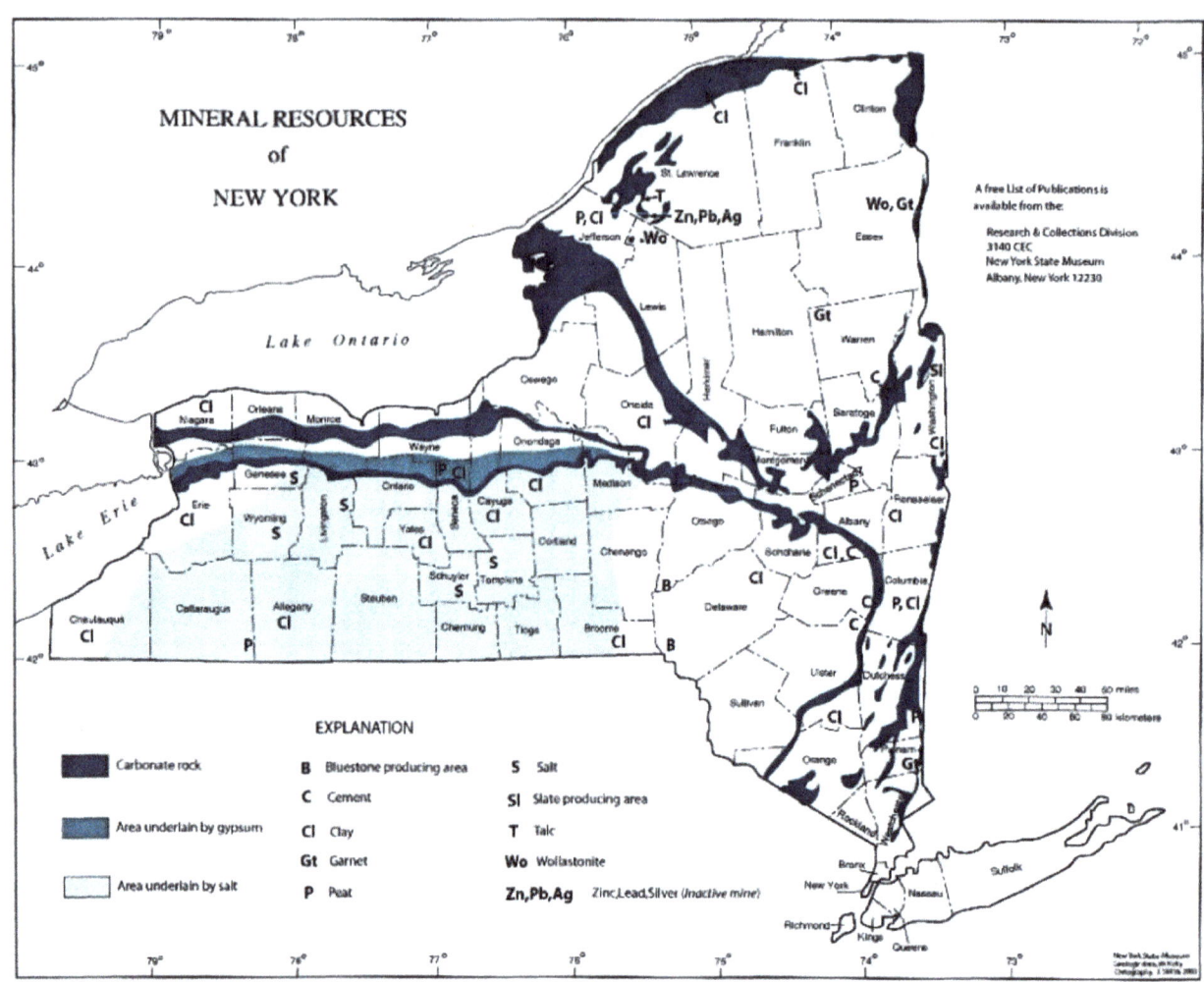

Map showing carbonate rocks in NYS including a belt that runs through Albany County. Source: DEC.

conducted a soils study of the Albany NY 15 Minute Quadrangle (That is topographical map talk) to classify the soils for engineering purposes. They looked at areas that would be considered geological hazards. The hazards were those areas having potential for landslides (read my recent piece on Troy landslides), sinkhole development, wind erosion and flood prone areas. Our concern here is sinkholes. The study revealed that sinkholes occur locally in soils that were laying on top of Devonian Onondaga and Helderberg Group limestone belts that extended from the south-central to north-central borders of the quad. Basically it is a shallow layer of glacial till sitting on top of bedrock. Clarksville has them from several feet to several hundred feet in size. New sinkholes are created when housing development, new roads, parking lots and such are built as they divert the water flow and or concentration of water in a particular region.

Schenectady GE scientist Charles Steinmetz and company enjoying dinner under this cave also caused by running water dissolving the carbonate rocks at Thacher Park. Photo Don Rittner.

It should be no surprise then that the potential for sinkholes is mostly in the western part of the quad in areas of New Scotland and Bethlehem, basically the Helderberg Mountain region. I would not expect though that you will see houses being swallowed up as it is pretty easy to divert the ground flow in areas where a small sinkhole can be observed. However, you never know what has been going on over the last few million years under the ground in that part of the Capital District.

Let's hope you never get that sinking feeling.

Albany has no problems destroying remnants of its Dutch culture or other historic buildings that helped give the city its character.

One of the oldest European cities in America founded by the Dutch in 1614 one would be hard pressed to find any remnants of Dutch culture. One surviving Dutch building on Hudson Avenue remains to be restored and perhaps become a center for learning about the beginning of American principles of democracy from its Dutch roots.

Above. The old Albany City Bank was taken down to make room for a bus stop. The Dutch house on the left was an example of several that still stood until the mid 1940s.

# Dear Albany – Why?
October 13, 2009 at 12:27 pm

There was quite an outcry about the lack of Albany officials greeting the 19 Dutch Flat-bottoms a few weeks ago. It even made the nightly news cast. I was thinking though really this is nothing new. Albany, and not to put the blame on any one person, has always scorned its history. When I was putting together one of my Albany history books a few years ago I found a passage that I included and will do so here. It was written by a young female student from the Girl's Academy, probably not older than 13, but older and wiser in so many ways. I bold face certain words. Take a read:

*"Albany, city of my birth! Ancient, yet new! Replete with interesting associations of the past, connected by so many links with the present, and promising to posterity a glorious future. Thy antique dwellings have been leveled, not so much by the ruthless hand of Time, as the merciless spirit of* **improvement.**

*Goths and Vandals! Ye were the sweet dispensers of the charities of life, compared to the demon who now stalks abroad under that abused name.*
*Where now are the palaces of the Knickerbockers and the Van Winkles? Gone! Leveled with the dust, or oh! worse,* **far** *worse, modernized!*

*Why the very Holland bricks — if they could speak, would cry shame! And the substantial beams fall down and crush the walls in their deep despair, when they are subjected to the degrading process of* **modernizing!**

*Shades of our fathers! Why is it permitted? To* **renovate**, *to* **preserve** *those remnants of the past, should be our pious aim, not with profane hands to cut, hew down, and alter the roof trees which have sheltered generation after generation."*
–The Monthly Rose, Albany Female Academy.

Want to know when it was written? In 1845!

Below is a cartoon I did back in 1983 with Raoul Vezina regarding Albany's preservation policy. Raoul and I were doing a weekly Naturalist At Large cartoon series in the old Knickerbocker News before his untimely death.

Albany's Preservation Policy, Cartoon by Don Rittner & Raoul Vezina, 1983.